MINAL
Lexington Avenue

BUILDINGS, ETC.

Ⓖ – Grand Central Art Galleries
Ⓗ – Office Space
Ⓙ – Main Waiting Room
Ⓚ – Restaurants
Ⓛ – 42nd Street Entrance
Ⓜ – Parcel Rooms, Shops, and Stores

GRAND CENTRAL

...the World's Greatest Railway Terminal

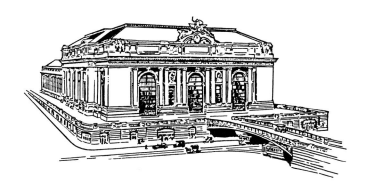

William D. Middleton

❖❖❖

Revised Edition 1999

❖❖❖

Golden West Books

· San Marino, California ·

GRAND CENTRAL

Copyright © 1977 by William D. Middleton

All Rights Reserved

Published by Golden West Books

San Marino, California 91108 U.S.A.

Library of Congress Catalog Card No. 77-24507

I.S.B.N. 0-87095-071-1

1st Printing - October 1977
2nd Printing - June 1978

Revised Edition
3rd Printing - May 1999

Library of Congress Cataloging in Publication Data

Middleton, William D.,   1923-
    Grand Central, the world's greatest railway terminal

    Bibliography: p.
    Includes index.
    1. New York. Grand Central Terminal.   I.   Title.
TF302.N7M53   385'.314' 097471   77-24507
ISBN 0-87095-071-1

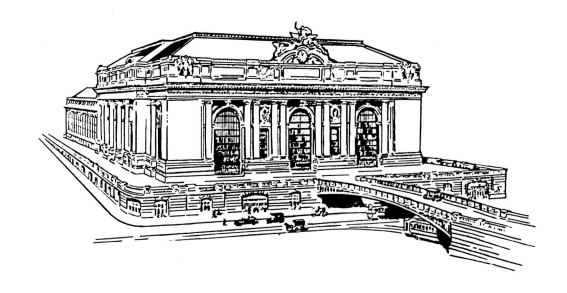

Golden West Books

P.O. Box 80250 • San Marino, California • 91118-8250

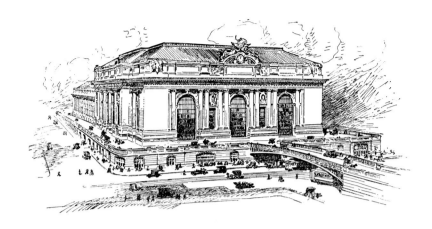

THE RAILROAD STATION

The station, as he entered it, was murmurous
With the immense and distant sound of time.
Great, slant beams of moted light
Fell ponderously athwart the station's floor,
And the calm voice of time
Hovered along the walls and ceiling
Of that mighty room,
Distilled out of the voices and movements
Of the people who swarmed beneath.

It had the murmur of a distant sea,
The languorous lapse and flow
Of waters on a beach.
It was elemental, detached,
Indifferent to the lives of men.

They contributed to it
As drops of rain contribute to a river
That draws its flood and movement
Majestically from great depths,
Out of purple hills at evening.

Few buildings are vast enough
To hold the sound of time,
And now it seemed to him
That there was a superb fitness in the fact
That the one which held it better than all others
Should be a railroad station.
For here, as nowhere else on earth,
Men were brought together for a moment
At the beginning or end
Of their innumerable journeys,
Here one saw their greetings and farewells,
Here, in a single instant,
One got the entire picture of the human destiny.
Men came and went, they passed and vanished,
And all were moving through the moments of
their lives
To death,
All made small tickings in the sound of time—
But the voice of time remained aloof and unper-
turbed,
A drowsy and eternal murmur
Below the immense and distant roof.
—*Thomas Wolfe*

"The Railroad Station" from *A Stone, A Leaf, A Door:* Poems by Thomas Wolfe, Selected and Arranged in Verse by John S. Barnes. Copyright 1945 by Maxwell Perkins as Executor (Charles Scribner's Sons). Originally in prose in *You Can't Go Home Again* by Thomas Wolfe. Copyright 1940 by Maxwell Perkins as Executor. By permission of Harper & Row, Publishers, Inc.

Foreword

New York's Grand Central Terminal was a product of that period spanning the turn of the century that was the golden age of the railroad passenger train. It was a time when the great and powerful railroad companies endeavored to surpass each other in the massive scale and opulence of their terminals; architectural historian Carroll L. V. Meeks called it the "megalomania" phase of station building.

"Such opulent dimensions were not functionally necessary," wrote Meeks of Grand Central and the rival Pennsylvania Station across town, "the companies could afford magnificence and enjoyed their munificent role, as princes had in predemocratic ages."

There were other stations from that era that enjoyed greater critical acclaim for the beauty of their architecture. Even in New York itself the Pennsylvania Railroad's huge Pennsylvania Station by McKim, Mead & White generally got higher marks from the architectural critics. Too, Grand Central was far from being the world's greatest terminal from the point of view of traffic. In 1913, for instance, the year Grand Central opened, Boston's South Station—then the busiest in the United States—handled almost three quarters again as many passengers as Grand Central, and more than twice as many trains.

But all of this was beside the point. For Grand Central Terminal was an extraordinary and unequalled merging of an inspired work of civil engineering, a landmark achievement for the still-young profession of electrical engineering, and a distinguished example of functional architecture. In the sheer, breathtaking magnitude of its overall scope, and the brilliance of its execution, the New York Central's great New York terminal project was unique. "No similar enterprise was ever undertaken on so gigantic a scale, or in the face of such conditions as have beset its builders," wrote Hugh Thompson of it in the April 1911 issue of *Munsey's Magazine*. And indeed, there was never to be another terminal project quite its equal.

But Grand Central was—and is—much more than just a great railroad terminal. For Grand Central was also a brilliant and pioneering work of urban development that has acted as the center and the catalyst for the dynamic development and growth of mid-town Manhattan for more than half a century. The first of its kind, Grand Central was the prototype for such multi-purpose urban centers as New York's Rockefeller Center project of the 1930's, and Montreal's downtown redevelopment centering around Central Station of the 1960's.

Even before the project was completed Grand

Central's great potential as an urban center was foreseen. "When you come to sum up the Grand Central Terminal as an accomplishment," concluded Hugh Thompson in his 1911 *Munsey's* article, "you find that it is much more than a railway-station. It will be a new city center; a vast theater for big events; another triumph of constructive American achievement."

Surely Grand Central has turned out to be all that and more.

Some may suggest that only a native New Yorker could properly write the story of Grand Central Terminal. Perhaps so, but I would suggest that no one can appreciate this splendid place any more than someone who grew up not knowing that such a wonderful place existed. My own acquaintance with Grand Central goes back fully three decades to the summer of 1946, coincidentally in what was to prove the zenith year of its existence as a passenger terminal, when I visited New York for the first time as a youth on my way to college in upstate New York. I can still remember taking the subway over from Penn Station (you followed the red lights in the Times Square shuttle to get from Penn Station to Grand Central, or the green lights the other way around) and walking, awe-stricken, into that great room. It seemed a place, as Thomas Wolfe wrote, of "great, slant beams of moted light" and "the murmur of a distant sea," a place "vast enough to hold the sound of time," and it made what has been an enduring impression.

Over the years of my fascination with Grand Central I have revisited it countless times, have sorrowed as its fortunes decline, and rejoiced—less often—as they advanced. Always it has been a place of endless fascination, on each visit revealing some delightful new facet of its innovative, brilliant design—a convenient passageway, a handsome piece of decorative work, or perhaps a new vantage point overlooking the great concourse. I don't think I have learned everything there is to know about Grand Central, and I doubt that I ever will.

For all who share with me the belief that Grand Central is a very special place, this volume is presented as an affectionate look back at the first century of Grand Central history, for the story is not confined just to that of the present "new" structure of 1903-13, but properly includes as well that of Commodore Vanderbilt's first Grand Central of 1869-71, and its reconstruction of 1898-1900. And perhaps at this point I should set the record straight as to the name. The first Grand Central was officially known as Grand Central *Depot*. The name was changed to Grand Central *Station* several years before the extensive alterations of 1898-1900, and the present structure is Grand Central *Terminal*. I know that almost everyone still calls it Grand Central Station, but *Terminal* is what's chiseled in Bedford limestone over the 42nd Street facade.

For a wide variety of assistance with both research and illustrative material I am greatly indebted to more than a score of individuals and institutions. Grand Central's General Station Master, Edward V. Quinn, Jr., and his assistant, William J. Haley, kindly guided me on my explorations of the labyrinthine back ways of the terminal building, while Terminal Train Master Dennis Healey showed me the world of switch points and signals beyond the platforms, and afforded me the rare treat of a trip around the lower level loop on foot. Cecil G. Muldoon, formerly the assistant director of public relations and advertising for Penn Central at 466 Lexington Avenue, assisted greatly in my research through the railroad's extensive Grand Central historical files, and his successor at what is now ConRail, William E. Baird, has been no less helpful. A. V. Marterelli, of Penn Central's Philadelphia headquarters, helped clear up some ambiguities of the beginnings of Manhattan railroads by making available early records of the New York & Harlem. For their assistance with diverse reference materials or suggestions I owe sincere thanks to Dr. Bernard L. Albert; Elliott Beckelman of The Committee to Save Grand Central Station; Alan Burnham, Director of Research for the Landmarks Preservation Commission of the City of New York; Jill M. Christopherson of the Minnesota Historical Society; Hall E. Downey of the General Railway Signal Co.; publisher Donald Duke; Donald O. Eisele; Arnold B. Joseph; Alan K. Lathrop, curator of the Manuscripts Division, University of Minnesota Libraries; Lola Preiss, public relations director of The Waldorf-Astoria; Ron Rosenberg; John H. White, Jr. of the Smithsonian Institution, and *The New Yorker* magazine's Rogers E. M. Whitaker, better known as E. M. Frimbo, the World's Greatest

Railroad Buff. I am particularly grateful for the help of Herbert H. Harwood and his son Herb, Jr., railroad men both, who generously made available valued photographs and other memorabilia relating to the work of their father and grandfather, George A. Harwood, in the construction of Grand Central Terminal. The research facilities of the Library of Congress and the New York Public Library have also proven particularly helpful. For the diversity and quality of this book's illustrative material I am fortunate to have had the assistance of photographer Jane F. Goldsmith; former New York Central photographer Ed Nowak, who himself took many of the railroad's splendid views of Grand Central included in these pages, and printed many others from the old NYC negative file; Joseph D. Thompson, who provided prints from Alco Historic Photos; the pictorial archives of the Library of Congress, the Museum of the City of New York, and the New York Public Library; and of the several other individuals and institutions whose contributions are individually credited. A particularly pleasant memory of the work on this book will always be that of an evening spent with the late Herman Rinke, who added immeasurably to my stock of Grand Central lore with his tales of ten years as a Grand Central towerman. A very special thanks is also due Herman, and New Yorkers Edward L. May, Francis J. Goldsmith, Jr. and Hugh A. Dunne, who kindly offered to read the manuscript and contributed greatly to its accuracy from their extensive knowledge of New York City's railroad history. Hugh Dunne has also been exceedingly generous with his time and effort in helping to clear up several questions concerning the early history of the New York & Harlem and the development of the Grand Central District. Any surviving errors, however, must remain my responsibility. Finally, I extend a very personal thanks to my wife Dorothy, who edited the manuscript with her usual technical skill and pungent wit and to "O" Fowler, who so competently typed it.

—*William D. Middleton*
Point Mugu, California

Table of Contents

Around 1851, soon after trains began running on the Hudson River Railroad, the company established this lower Manhattan terminal at Chambers Street and West Broadway. Steam locomotives were taken off the trains at 33rd Street, and the cars were then hauled through the streets by horses for the remaining distance of nearly three miles to Chambers and West Broadway.—PENN CENTRAL COMPANY

1

The Railroad Comes to Manhattan

One day it would grow into one of the greatest of all American railroads, and its splendid fleet of passenger trains would arrive and depart from a magnificent station on 42nd Street that would be called, with no exaggeration, the "greatest railroad terminal in the world." But, however mighty an engine of transport it was finally to become, the coming of the railroad to Manhattan a century and a half ago was marked by the most humble of beginnings. Surely few enterprises were ever more appropriately described by the expression "mighty things from small beginnings grow."

By 1830 New York, with a population in excess of 200,000, had become both the nation's largest city and the center of American commerce. The city's commercial pre-eminence was firmly founded on its access to an unparalleled system of water transportation. A superb natural harbor gave New York a dominant position in both coastal and transatlantic shipping. Flourishing steamboat ser-

vices operating on the Hudson River linked the city and its harbor with upstate New York and the Great Lakes via the new Erie Canal, completed in 1825.

The first regular steam operation of railroads in North America began in 1830, and that event marked the beginning of a great era of growth and expansion for the American railroad. New railroad enterprises sprang up on all sides; by the end of the decade there would be nearly 3,000 miles of track in operation in North America.

For all its importance as a center of water transport, New York City, too, would have its new railroad.

That first railroad had exceedingly modest objectives. Organized by a group of New York businessmen, and chartered by the New York Legislature on August 25, 1831, the New York & Harlem Railroad Company* was limited by its charter to Manhattan Island, being empowered to build a line between Third and Eighth avenues from any point on the north

side of 23rd Street to any point on the Harlem River, at the upper end of Manhattan, with a branch to the Hudson River between 124th and 129th streets. New York was then confined to the lower end of the island, and the city's projected street system had not yet been opened north of 34th Street. The community of Harlem, the railroad's northern objective, was 6½ miles away across Manhattan's rugged mid-island terrain, with only the hamlet of Yorkville lying between.

Finding 23rd Street to be too far north for the road's southern terminal, the railroad obtained an amended authority in 1832 that permitted it to operate farther south, to Prince Street.

Construction work began on February 23, 1832, at a rocky section of Murray Hill, and the first trip was operated over the line in November of the same year. Drawn by horses, the cars ran over a line of less than a mile over the Bowery** from Prince Street north to

Union Square, at 14th Street. In reality, this first section of the New York & Harlem was no more than a streetcar line; indeed, its opening is celebrated as the first American street railway.

A crowd of some 60 distinguished guests assembled to ride the cars on an initial southbound run over the line on the afternoon of November 14th. According to an account in the *Morning Courier and Enquirer:*

"The Harlem Railroad Company with the Mayor, Corporation, and strangers of distinction, left the City Hall in carriages to the place of depot near Union Square, where two splendid cars made by Milne Parker, each with two horses, were in waiting. These cars are made low with broad iron wheels which fit the flanges of the railroad after an improved model from the Liverpool and Manchester cars. They resemble an omnibus, or rather several omnibuses attached to each other, padded with fine cloth and handsome glass windows, each capable of containing, outside and inside, fully forty passengers. The company was soon seated and the horses trotted off in handsome style, with great ease, at the rate of about twelve miles, followed by a number

*The name of the railroad originally appeared as the New York & Harlaem, in deference to the Dutch spelling of the community name then common, but the shorter spelling soon became standard for both the place and the railroad.

**A section of what was then known as the Bowery, from Union Square to 4th Street, is known today as Fourth Avenue.

of private barouches and horsemen. Groups of spectators greeted the passengers of the cars with shouts and every window in the Bowery was filled.

"After the experiment, the company and guests dined at the City Hotel and terminated, in a very agreeable manner, the first essay of New Yorkers on a railroad in their own city."

Soon, predicted the newspaper, New York's citizens would no longer be cramped and confined in the city, but would be able to enjoy a comfortable house on an acre or two of land, with "a garden, orchard, dairy, and other conveniences." Harlem, it was even ventured, would be made a suburb of New York.

Gradually the new railroad worked its way northward in Fourth Avenue. Service was opened to 32nd Street in June 1833. Following completion of a difficult rock cut at Murray Hill, on Fourth Avenue between 32nd and 41st streets, the cars began running as far north as 85th Street, Yorkville, early in May of 1834. Completion of the line to Harlem was a difficult task, requiring the boring of the 596-foot Mt. Prospect tunnel through the heights at Observatory Place, between 92nd and 94th streets. One of the first American railroad tunnels, it proved to be quite a curiosity, drawing many passengers to the line just for the novel experience of riding through it. The tunnel complete, service was finally opened all the way to 125th Street, Harlem, late in 1837. Traffic developed rapidly, and the railroad was soon obliged to begin the construction of a second track.

For the first few years the New York & Harlem was operated entirely with horses as its motive power. After several tests, the company bought its first steam locomotive around 1837. Others were added to the motive power fleet over the next few years. Because of restrictions imposed by its charter, however, the railroad was obliged to operate exclusively with horse power below 14th Street.

What may have been Manhattan's first railroad station was opened by the New York & Harlem early in 1833, when the railroad rented an office on the Bowery and in turn let it to a Joseph B. Roe for the sale of passenger tickets on its trains, for which Roe was to receive a 5 percent commission.

In 1837 the railroad established its offices and stables on 4th Avenue, between 26th and 27th streets. Somewhat later a station was constructed here, and this location then became the southern terminal for steam locomotive operation. Another station was established in Tryon Row in 1839, after the railroad completed the construction of an extension southward as far as City Hall.

According to its original charter, the New York & Harlem was to confine its operations to the island of Manhattan, but almost from the beginning the company's organizers had their eye on more ambitious objectives. Originally, these objectives centered around the New York & Albany Railroad, a projected line that was to extend north from a terminal at the Harlem River to an eventual northern terminal at Albany.

The New York & Albany was chartered on April 17, 1832, with several of the New York & Harlem's promoters among its incorporators, but the project never did materialize. Finally, in 1840, the New York & Harlem acquired a broadened charter, assumed most of the powers originally granted to the stillborn New York & Albany, and commenced building north from the Harlem River on its own. Trains were running to Fordham by 1841, and to White Plains by the end of 1844. By the beginning of 1852, the Harlem had completed its line all the way to a junction with the Western Railroad of Massachusetts, later the Boston & Albany, at what is now Chatham,

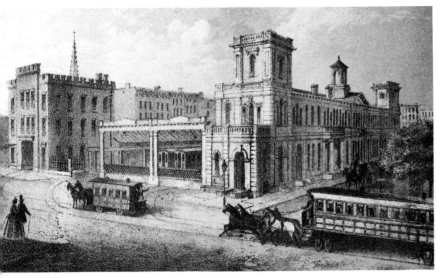

New York's first railroad terminal of real consequence was this joint station on Fourth Avenue between 26th and 27th streets. The structure on the right, on the 27th Street side, housed the facilities of the New York & New Haven, while that on the left was occupied by the New York & Harlem. By the time this lithograph was made for *D. T. Valentine's Manual* in 1860, the railroads were obliged to terminate steam locomotive operation at 42nd Street, where trains were then broken up and the cars hauled the remainder of the distance to the Fourth Avenue station by teams of horses.—LIBRARY OF CONGRESS

This woodcut by engravers Purcell & Dutton, made about 1860, shows brisk street traffic activitiy outside the New Haven depot at 27th Street and Fourth Avenue. —THE J. CLARENCE DAVIES COLLECTION, MUSEUM OF THE CITY OF NEW YORK

New York, some 131 miles north of Manhattan, and began running through cars to Albany. Encouraging increases in traffic were soon felt from the extensions, particularly in the form of commuter traffic from the new towns and villages that sprang up in The Bronx following completion of the line.

Construction of the New York & Harlem north of the Harlem River also afforded a second railroad, the New York & New Haven, an opportunity to gain a direct entrance to Manhattan.

The New York & New Haven had been chartered in 1844 to build a line between the two cities that would complete a through railroad route between Boston and New York. In 1845 the New York & New Haven had applied to the New York Legislature for the necessary authority to build its own entrance into New York City. This move was successfully opposed by the New York & Harlem, and the New England company was then obliged to negotiate with the Harlem for trackage rights into the city.

A connection between the two roads was completed north of Williams Bridge, near what is now Mount Vernon, in December 1848, and through service between New York and Boston, operating via Springfield, Massachusetts, was started early the following year. The New Haven opened its own station on lower

Manhattan at 29 Canal Street, near Broadway. Cars were pulled by horses as far north as the Harlem's station at 27th Street, where additional passengers were taken on and steam locomotives replaced the animal power.

Not quite a decade later, in 1857, the two roads moved their principal Manhattan passenger stations to new facilities installed side-by-side on the Fourth Avenue site between 26th and 27th streets. Occupying the entire block on the west side of Fourth Avenue, the joint stations extended back to Madison Avenue, just north of Madison Square, and had a total of 12 tracks.

Tracks led in from Fourth Avenue between the two nearly identical station buildings. Twin columns, standing about 25 feet high midway on the Fourth Avenue front, marked the boundary between the tracks of the two railroad companies. An architrave resting atop these twin columns extended above gates on either side, supported by single columns at its opposite ends. The gates, which were raised to give passage to arriving or departing trains, were intended to help restrict entry to the train yard to only those holding tickets. This arrangement caused some complaint from those coming to see friends off, but the railroads allowed that "the fine saloons of the depot afforded the best and most suitable facilities for shaking hands and the exchange of more affectionate adieus."

Although it was not nearly as large as the stations in such major railroad centers as Boston, Baltimore, or Chicago, the new Madison Square station was a handsome, towered structure that was the source of considerable pride for New Yorkers. Some 8,000 daily passengers arrived or departed from the joint stations, and the two roads operated more than 30 trains each way daily.

Almost from the time of the New York & Harlem's opening in 1832, the operation of steam locomotives through the streets of Manhattan constituted a source of increasing annoyance as both street and railroad traffic growth paralleled that of the city. From the very beginning, of course, the operation of steam power had been prohibited below 14th Street. The explosion of a locomotive boiler at Union Square and 15th Street on July 4, 1839, which killed the engineer and injured 20

persons, led to even stronger opposition to the use of steam power, and in 1844 the Common Council and the Mayor ordered the Harlem to discontinue the operation of steam locomotives below 32nd Street. The following year the railroad established an engine house at Fourth Avenue and 32nd Street, but even this location proved a temporary one. By the end of 1858 a further action of the Council and Mayor had pushed the southern limit for steam power operation northward to a new locomotive terminal just north of 42nd Street. Trains were broken up here and teams of horses pulled the individual cars for the remainder of the distance to the terminal at Madison Square.

An interesting account of railroad travel out of New York in the days of the Madison Square station is provided by Inglis Stuart, writing in the *Bulletin* of the Railway & Locomotive Historical Society in 1926. As a small boy Stuart had accompanied his mother on a journey from New York to Pittsfield, Massachusetts, over the New Haven road in 1865.

According to Stuart's recollection, there was no restaurant in the station, but this was of no great consequence, for hungry passengers had only to cross Fourth Avenue to Lawrence R. Kerr's Putnam House, which was noted for its substantial and excellent fare. A large punch bowl in the window was always heaped with the doughnuts for which the Putnam was famous. Light meals were also available a few doors up the street at Ellis' Bakery.

The cars in use then were a mixture of the older flat-topped type and the newer monitor-roofed variety. The New York & Harlem cars were painted dark blue or pea green, while the New Haven favored what Stuart called a straw color. Describing the departure of a train, he wrote:

"When a train was ready to depart, the gate shot up and horses attached to the car pulled it through the gateway and around the abrupt curve into Fourth Avenue.... Rubbing of wheel flange against rail flange yielded a loud, clear, ringing sound.

"Northward along Fourth Avenue the four horses struck a gait of seven miles an hour. They were sturdy animals, manifesting zeal in duty and the leaders' arched necks displayed pride in their jingling bells. The driver held a short whip

carrying a long lash which now and again he would spin into the air and check with a terrific crack.

"Following the baggage car, the remaining units of our train did not linger but departed in succession. Seated comfortably, there had fallen on our ears the warning, 'All Aboard!' What a tessitura that clarion voice revealed!... And so our car, not loitering, took to flight and kissing the curve warbled that ringing aria. Merrily we rolled along Fourth Avenue to the harmony of hoof beats on the cobbles, jingling bells, detonations of the whip, and shrill cries of gamins hopping on for a joy ride....

"Our caravan, keeping its pace, entered Murray Hill Tunnel. Through these gloomy precincts, feebly lighted by kerosene lamps on brackets and with a din from many noisemaking factors, our car roared on to sunlight at Forty-second Street. Crossing this thoroughfare, the 'Yard' was attained.... And here awaiting us... stood our New Haven locomotive, humming under full pressure—eager to speed away.

"It was fascinating... to witness the speed and precision with which the cars, one after another, were linked into a train. As a car from Twenty-sixth or Twenty-seventh Street neared the locomotive, the driver, holding in his left hand reins and whip, with his right reached down the three foot hook which was part of his outfit and with it caught the team pole. As his hook caught, the brakeman at his side leaned to lift the pin. As the pin came up, the driver shouted to his horses and they sharply swerved from the track, while he, still grasping reins and whip and holding up

the team pole, strode down the steps and sprang to the ground. The brakeman now turned the wheel to retard. So neatly did he gauge that the coupling link protruding from the tender came gently within the jaw and at that instant he dropped the pin into the drawhead. Then straightening, he reached overhead with one hand for the bell cord, in the same movement catching with his other hand the cord which the foreman, Gaucho style, twirled from the cab. Snapping the ends together, the brakeman bolted down the steps and raced rearward to board the next on-coming car. Upon the platform of this the manoeuvres just described were re-enacted. Thus unit after unit was coupled forming an assembled train....

"Again that clarion voice from somewhere outside: 'All Right There?' and a moment later came two trumpet notes from the whistle followed by a jerk as slack was taken up from car to car. Leaving the confines of the 'Yard,' our engineer played that long bravura... and we spun along an airline track to Harlem River...."

The New York & Harlem had hardly begun to lay track north of the Harlem River, with a link to Albany as its eventual goal, when a new railroad appeared on the scene to stake a claim to an alternate route between New York and Albany.

When the New York & Harlem and its projected New York & Albany connection were first contemplated in the early 1830's, the idea of competing directly with the powerful Hudson River steamboat lines seemed foolhardy in the extreme. Beginning with the celebrated run of Robert Fulton's *Clermont* between New York and Albany in 1807, the steamboat industry on the Hudson had grown rapidly. Originally, the monopoly founded by Fulton and Robert R. Livingston had dominated the river trade, but by 1840 there were no less than five lines competing on the New York-Albany run alone. Steamboats by the dozen plied the waters of the Hudson daily.

In the face of this waterborne competition, the New York & Harlem stayed well away from the river, building its line north through Brewster and Pawling to Chatham, leaving the communities along the east bank of the Hudson to the steamboat men.

This state of affairs was not to everyone's liking. For most of the year the Hudson River communities enjoyed the low cost transportation afforded by the fiercely competitive steamboat lines, but the period of several months each winter when the river was either frozen solid or so choked with ice that the boats were unable to run constituted a significant impediment to trade. And as the new railroads became increasingly common elsewhere, businessmen in the river towns also began to fear that their communities might be bypassed by trade.

Some of the strongest sentiment for a railroad along the Hudson was centered in Poughkeepsie, and it was a group of Poughkeepsie businessmen that in 1846 finally succeeded in getting a charter from the New York Legislature for the construction of the Hudson River Railroad, which would follow the east bank of the Hudson from New York to Albany. John B. Jervis, a noted civil engineer, was engaged as chief engineer and construction was started the following year. By the end of 1849 trains were operating from New York as far north as Poughkeepsie. Despite the extraordinarily difficult construction problems

encountered in building along the Hudson, the entire line was completed and regular service started between New York and Albany at the beginning of October 1851. So rapidly had the line been built that its opening actually preceded by several months the completion of the older New York & Harlem's inland route which reached Albany by way of Chatham.

The Hudson River Railroad reached its New York terminal via a route along the west shore of Manhattan. Initially, trains ran from a station at 31st Street, but soon afterward the railroad obtained permission to extend its tracks to lower Manhattan through Tenth Avenue and West, Canal, and Hudson streets. A downtown terminal was constructed at Chambers Street and West Broadway. The Hudson River Railroad, just like the Harlem, was required by the city to pull its cars through the streets with horses. Steam locomotives were put on or taken off trains at an engine terminal at 33rd Street. In later years a sort of shrouded locomotive usually referred to as a "dummy," and preceded by a man on horseback with a red flag, was used to pull trains south of 30th Street.

Titled "Field Sports of New York—Car Racing on the Bowery," this lurid drawing of a New York & Harlem mishap appeared in an 1865 issue of *Frank Leslie's Illustrated Newspaper* as part of a more or less continuing campaign against reckless horsecar operation carried on by *Leslie's*. The operation of steam locomotives through the streets of New York was even less popular, and the railroad's southern terminal of steam operation was gradually forced northward from 14th Street to 42nd Street.—LIBRARY OF CONGRESS

17

A little more than a decade after the Hudson River Railroad began running, the company completed a new terminal at Tenth Avenue and 30th Street. Although it was to be the railroad's principal Manhattan terminal, it was described by the New York *Tribune* as "not a very imposing structure." Constructed of brick, it was 200 feet long and 28 feet wide. There were separate entrances and waiting rooms for ladies and gentlemen, separated by a ticket office in the center of the building. Other facilities included a telegraph office, a baggage room, and a refreshment room above the ticket office.

The new 30th Street station was rushed to completion early in 1861 in time for the arrival in New York of President-elect Abraham Lincoln, en route from Springfield, Illinois, to his inauguration at Washington. After an overnight stop at Albany, Mr. Lincoln and his party left for New York by special train on the morning of February 19th, arriving at 30th Street promptly at 3 P.M. behind the Hudson River Railroad's locomotive *Constitution*. A huge flag, 20 feet by 14 feet, flew above the station in honor of its distinguished first passenger, and a large party greeted the President-elect at a reception in the station's waiting room, after which Lincoln and his party proceeded to their accommodations at the Astor House.

On a far more melancholy occasion scarcely four years later, on April 25, 1865, the Hudson River depot saw the departure of the funeral train bearing the body of the martyred Lincoln back home to Springfield. The President's funeral train had arrived at Jersey City the previous morning. The casket had been ferried across the Hudson on the ferry *New York* to Desbrosses Street, and then taken to the New York City Hall, where it had lain in state until the afternoon of the 25th. The casket was then carried through the streets to the 30th Street station, where the Seventh Regiment was lined up as a Guard of Honor. Promptly at 4 P.M. the funeral train, its seven cars draped in black, pulled slowly away from the depot. At its head was the *Union*, one of the same Hudson River Railroad locomotives that had pulled the President-elect's train on its triumphal journey east in 1861.

Illustrative of the conflict between locomotive-drawn trains and other traffic in the increasingly congested New York streets is this newspaper drawing of a collision on Manhattan's West Side between a New York Central & Hudson River train and a Belt Line horse car. The man and woman, we are told, were mangled, but not killed.—COURTESY OF RAILROAD MAGAZINE

By the end of the Civil War the United States was well-embarked on its great age of railroad expansion. New England and the states of the Northeast were already well-served by their growing networks of railroad lines. Through their connections the lines out of New York reached as far west as the Mississippi River and beyond. In the West the nation was embarked on the great adventure of the Pacific Railroad that by 1869 would complete an unbroken link of rails from the Atlantic to the Pacific.

Seeing in this great age of American railroads an opportunity for enormous profit, a powerful new figure now came on the scene at New York. First acquiring control of the New York & Harlem and then the Hudson River Railroad, millionaire steamboat tycoon Cornelius Vanderbilt soon built them into the cornerstone of a great railroad system that would ultimately stretch all the way from the Atlantic to the Great Lakes and the Middle West. And within less than a decade New York's railroads and their Manhattan terminals would undergo a most remarkable transformation.

Only a few months after it opened, Commodore Vanderbilt's splendid new Grand Central Depot was delineated by woodcut artist S. Fox for readers of the February 3, 1872 issue of *Harper's Weekly*. The Second Empire style building was patterned after the Tuileries at Paris and was finished in red brick and cast iron trim, painted white to resemble marble. This view faces the 42nd Street and Vanderbilt Avenue corner of the building.—NEW YORK PUBLIC LIBRARY

2

The Commodore's Palace on 42nd Street

Cornelius Vanderbilt was perhaps the greatest of all that 19th century band of brilliant, shrewd—and ruthless—entrepreneurs that helped to make the United States into a world power in business and industry. Born on Staten Island, New York, in 1794, Vanderbilt came from a family of exceedingly modest means, and he enjoyed little formal schooling. Yet when he died in 1877 at the age of 82, Vanderbilt was the richest man in America, leaving a fortune of some $105 million.

For the first half-century of his adult life, Cornelius Vanderbilt was a steamboat man; it was as a young man in the boating business that he acquired the nickname "Commodore" that was to stick with him all his life. Young Vanderbilt started out in business at the age of 16 with a *periauger*—a little sailing boat— hauling farm produce and passengers across New York Harbor. By the 1850's he had parlayed this modest enterprise into a great shipping empire. Vanderbilt steamboats oper-

ated on the Hudson River and up the coast to Providence and Boston, his ocean-going steamships operated as far afield as San Francisco and Le Havre, and Cornelius Vanderbilt was a millionaire at least ten times over.

Like any good steamboat man, Vanderbilt had little use for the upstart railroads. As late as 1857, when a friend attempted to interest him in the New York & Harlem, he is said to have replied, "Bring me a steamboat and I can do something, but I won't have anything to do with your damn railroads," or something like that. But only a few years later, at the age of 70, Commodore Vanderbilt decided to sell off his ships and began accumulating railroads as eagerly as he had once acquired steamboats.

Vanderbilt's change of heart about railroads was based on a shrewd recognition that the growth of the nation then spreading westward into the Great Plains would no longer follow the waterways of canal and river, but would now be sustained by steel rails. And in the last dozen years of his life Cornelius Vanderbilt set

Already 70 years old when he entered the railroad business, Commodore Cornelius Vanderbilt assembled one of the greatest railroad systems of the 19th Century and crowned his system with the finest railroad station in the Western Hemisphere. This photograph was taken by Mathew Brady, whose pictorial record of the Civil War was to make him one of the best-known of all U.S. Photographers.—SIGNAL CORPS, BRADY COLLECTION, NATIONAL ARCHIVES

out to dominate that coming American railroad age by building the greatest American railroad empire of the 19th century.

The Commodore's first railroad acquisition, in 1863, was the New York & Harlem. The Harlem was then in a not very healthy state and with the help of some of the behind-the-scenes maneuvering at which he was so well-practiced, Vanderbilt was able to gain control of the railroad at a bargain price of $9 a share. Next, only a year later, the Commodore bought a controlling interest in the rival Hudson River Railroad.

A third railroad was added to the Vanderbilt empire in 1867 after a piece of corporate buccaneering that is illustrative of the Commodore's methods at their best, or worst, depending on how one looks at it.

In 1866 Vanderbilt had acquired a large block of stock in the New York Central Railroad, which then extended across New York State from Albany to Buffalo, but he had

been unsuccessful in an attempt to take control of the property.

During most of the year, freight and passengers from the Central would continue on to New York City from Albany either on board Hudson River steamboats or over Commodore Vanderbilt's Hudson River Railroad. During the winter months, however, the river was frozen over and only the Commodore's trains were available. The shrewd Vanderbilt soon devised a scheme to take advantage of this dependence and to use it to wrest control of the Central for himself. In January 1867 Vanderbilt's Hudson River Railroad simply notified the Central that it would no longer accept traffic from it. Hudson River trains no longer crossed the Hudson River bridge into Albany. Passengers were obliged to walk across the bridge through the snow, dragging their baggage with them, and often arriving at the Hudson River road's station only to find that their train had already

Commodore Vanderbilt's eldest son, William H. Vanderbilt, was one of his father's most trusted lieutenants in the management of the great Vanderbilt railroad empire. As a vice-president of both the New York & Harlem and the New York Central & Hudson River, the younger Vanderbilt gave general directions to the construction of the Grand Central Depot.—PENN CENTRAL COMPANY

departed. Freight began piling up in Albany and shippers soon were routing their freight from Buffalo to New York City over the rival Erie Railroad. New York Central earnings quickly declined and the price of the road's stock began to fall. As Central stock prices went down, Vanderbilt quickly increased his holdings. Before the year was out the Central's remaining stockholders saw the light and offered Vanderbilt control of the railroad.

Within the next few years Vanderbilt completed the assembly of his great New York to Chicago railroad empire with the purchase of controlling interests in the Lake Shore & Michigan Southern Railroad, between Buffalo and Chicago, and of the Canada Southern and Michigan Central railroads, which afforded a second Buffalo-Chicago route via southern Ontario. Millions of dollars were lavished on the rebuilding of these lines into a first class rail system that soon became the dominant carrier between New York and Chicago.

Meanwhile, Vanderbilt had set out to consolidate his New York rail holdings. In 1869 the New York Legislature dutifully provided him with a bill that permitted the merger of the Hudson River and New York Central railroads into the New York Central and Hudson River Railroad (and simultaneously paved the way for a gigantic stock watering scheme). Even before this merger was carried out, work had started on projects that would consolidate the New York terminal facilities of the Hudson River and the Harlem lines.

The west side route of the Hudson River Railroad was to become the principal entry to Manhattan for freight traffic from the Vanderbilt lines. A full city block was acquired at St. John's Park, just south of Canal Street, on which Vanderbilt erected a huge four story brick freight house in 1868.

Similarly, the New York passenger terminal facilities of both Vanderbilt roads and the tenant New Haven were to be combined at a single splendid new terminal. The New York & Harlem, with its Fourth Avenue entrance to the heart of Manhattan, held the key to a consolidated terminal project, and the site selected for Vanderbilt's new Grand Central Depot, as it was to be called*, was that of the Harlem's existing steam locomotive facil-

ities between 42nd and 45th streets.

There were many who said the 42nd Street location was much too far uptown from the city's business center and its principal hotels. Indeed, it took something like 45 minutes to get from City Hall to 42nd Street on the Harlem's Fourth Avenue horse cars. But 42nd Street had its advantages, too. One of New York's extra-wide cross-town streets, it was recently paved with cobblestones. By this time, too, New York's population was approaching a million, and the city was rapidly growing northward on Manhattan. Before long, Vanderbilt reasoned, 42nd Street would no longer be too far uptown. In any case, both the lack of suitable real estate farther south and the City Council's prohibition against steam locomotive operation south of 42nd Street that had been in effect since 1859 effectively precluded serious consideration of a lower Manhattan site.

To gain access to the Grand Central Depot for trains from his New York Central & Hudson River, Vanderbilt had organized the Spuyten Duyvil & Port Morris Railroad in 1869. This road then constructed a line of some 7 miles along Spuyten Duyvil Creek and the east bank of the Harlem River which linked the tracks of the Hudson River road at Spuyten Duyvil with those of the Harlem at Mott Haven. The work cost nearly $1 million, and as soon as it was completed in 1871 the Spuyten Duyvil & Port Morris was leased to the NYC&HR and eventually—in 1913— merged with it.

South of Mott Haven, of course, all three railroads shared the Harlem's tracks for a distance of some 5 miles into the Grand Central Depot. To accommodate this great traffic the doubling of the line from two to four tracks, as well as the construction of extensive other improvements, was planned. Subsequently, in 1873, the Harlem line was leased to the New York Central & Hudson River, and was operated thereafter as a division of the larger company.

---

*In some early literature the new terminal was referred to as the "Grand Union Depot," but Grand Central Depot seems to have been its preferred title from the very beginning.

This view, dating from about 1870, shows the erection of the 100-foot-radius wrought iron arches that supported the vault of Grand Central Depot's splendid train shed.—PENN CENTRAL COMPANY

Construction was virtually complete when the above photograph of the great train shed was taken, probably in the fall of 1871 shortly before Grand Central opened to traffic. The photographer was facing the head house at the south end of the shed, where the New Haven's ticket office and waiting room were located. (LEFT) A close-up view of the base of the wrought iron arches in Grand Central's newly completed train shed shows their elaborately detailed cast iron tracery. It was a much-admired decorative feature of the terminal. (OPPOSITE PAGE) A view at the north end of Grand Central Depot around the time of its completion in 1871 shows the elaborate curtain wall of iron and glass that enclosed this end of the train shed. Somewhat reminiscent of the "false front" buildings of the Old West, it was often criticized for the way in which it hid the great arch of the train shed. Part way up the wall at the center can be seen the pulpit-like cabin from which the terminal dispatcher controlled the flow of traffic.—ALL PENN CENTRAL COMPANY

To the property already owned by the Harlem at the 42nd Street and Fourth Avenue site, Vanderbilt added additional land between Madison and Lexington avenues and extending as far north as 48th Street to provide sufficient room for the new terminal and its supporting yards and other facilities. The necessary authorization for the construction was obtained from the State of New York in May 1869, and the first foundation stone was laid on the following September 1.

Construction of the new station took more than two years, and the project cost the Commodore somewhere around $3 million. The work was carried out under the general direction of Vanderbilt and his son, William H. "Billy" Vanderbilt, who was then a vice-president of the Harlem. Isaac C. Buckhout, the Harlem's chief engineer, was responsible for engineering design of the project, and supervised the construction.

The most notable feature of the new depot was its great train shed, which emulated the design of the even larger shed at St. Pancras Station in London, constructed between 1863 and 1865. Cylindrical in cross section, Grand Central's huge train shed spanned 200 feet, rose to a height of 100 feet, and extended a length of 600 feet. It was supported by thirty semi-circular arched Howe trusses of wrought iron, each of which was tied together at the base by a wrought iron rod enclosed in a pipe placed under the surface of the tracks. Longitudinal trusses spanning between the arches

In another magnificent woodcut by artist S. Fox for the February 3, 1872, *Harper's Weekly* we are shown the interior of the train shed at Grand Central soon after its opening. The great structure was the largest interior space on the continent at the time, and architectural historians have ranked it as one of the 19th century's most important advances in building design.—NEW YORK PUBLIC LIBRARY

acted as stiffeners for the vault, which was sheathed in corrugated iron and lighted by three glazed monitors running the full length of the train shed. At night the shed was illuminated by a dozen large gas-fired chandeliers, which could be ignited automatically by an electric spark. Designed by engineer R. G. Hatfield, the great train shed was fabricated and erected by the Architectural Iron Works of New York.

The train shed spanned twelve tracks and five broad platforms, raised slightly above the track level. Ten of the tracks were stub-ended, while the two easternmost tracks extended entirely through the station to continue south in Fourth Avenue to the old station at 27th Street.

The north end of the shed was covered by an elaborate glass and iron curtain wall, with an arched opening for each track enclosed by a roll-up sheet iron door. Along its east side the

shed was enclosed by a brick wall about 30 feet in height.

On its west and south sides the train shed was enclosed by an L-shaped building which housed passenger facilities of the three railroads in a combination head and one-sided station. Designed by architect John B. Snook, the ornate depot—said to have been copied from the Tuileries in Paris—extended 249 feet along 42nd Street and 698 feet along the newly-created Vanderbilt Avenue. The building's elaborate Second Empire facade was finished in rich, red pressed brick, with ornamental coins, cornices, and window frames of cast iron, painted white in imitation of marble. Five ornate mansard-roofed towers surmounted the 42nd Street and Vanderbilt Avenue facades. Separate waiting and baggage rooms for the New York Central & Hudson River and the Harlem roads were provided in the Vanderbilt Avenue wing of the

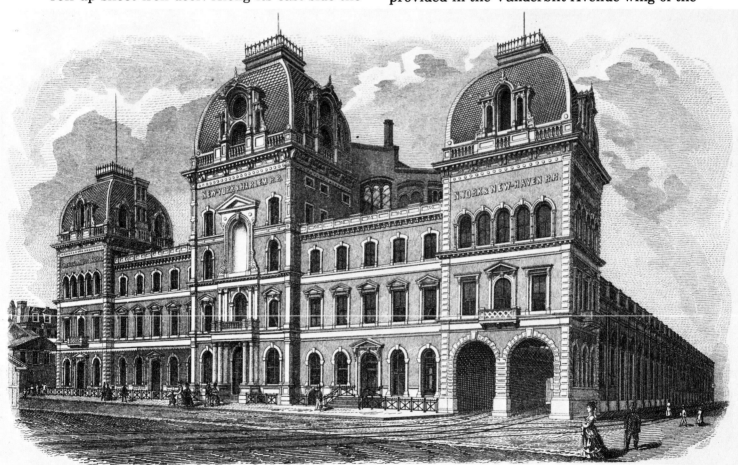

This 1871 view of the newly-completed depot from the southeast corner of Fourth Avenue and 42nd Street shows clearly the openings in the east tower which permitted the New York & Harlem's City cars to continue south through Fourth Avenue. The large niche at the third floor level of the center tower was evidently provided for the later installation of a statue, but was never used.

—NEW YORK PUBLIC LIBRARY

This view of the train shed, facing north from the head house, probably dates from the first year of operation. Visible on the right are local horse cars of the New York & Harlem that continued to operate south on Fourth Avenue for several years. In one of the old Grand Central's more spectacular mishaps, during New York's great blizzard of January 1877, the train shed roof became over-loaded with snow and the glass skylight gave way, showering the platforms with broken glass and ice. Miraculously, no one was injured.—PENN CENTRAL COMPANY

building, while the tenant New Haven somehow managed to acquire the preferred 42nd Street location for its separate waiting and baggage rooms. The upper floors of the three-story building were given over to offices for the railroad companies.

Although the Grand Central Depot was surpassed by several of the great European stations of its time, it was judged by architectural historian Carroll L. V. Meeks as the first American station "capable of standing comparison with the finest European ones." Its great train shed was the largest interior space on this continent and was ranked as a sight-seeing attraction second only to the National Capitol in Washington.

The new depot was generally received with great enthusiasm from the press and public. In its issue of June 30, 1871, for example, the *New York Herald* called it "the largest railway and passenger caravansary in the world," and exclaimed over its "one thousand miles of railroad centering in a ferruginous palace."

Even in its own time, however, Vanderbilt's Grand Central Depot was not universally admired. Its architectural treatment was variously described by critics as unattractive and "fussy," and the exterior color scheme as "unfortunate." The soaring arch of the depot's most notable feature, the great iron train shed, was effectively hidden from view at one end by the depot building and at the other end by the iron curtain wall whose elaborate, gabled profile bore little resemblance to the curve of the train shed arch.

In several important respects the station's passenger facilities turned out to have been extremely ill-designed. So thoroughly had the waiting rooms of the three railroads been separated that passengers changing from one road to another were obliged to leave the building and enter by another door. Arriving passengers had no access to the waiting rooms at all, but were channeled directly to the sidewalks, where there was no shelter provided against rain, snow, or other vagaries of the weather. The incoming baggage room was so located that it opened out into the train shed, making it necessary for a passenger to show a railroad ticket in order to claim his baggage.

In any event, the Grand Central Depot was one of the greatest American stations of the 19th century, and it was a structure sufficiently grand and pretentious even for Commodore Vanderbilt, who—as Meeks put it—"was undoubtedly vain enough to feel that there was nothing incongruous in transplanting a palace to serve as his personal headquarters."

After all, Commodore Vanderbilt was the kind of man who once proposed to erect a memorial in Central Park, larger even than the Washington Monument, which would jointly commemorate George Washington and himself, and had gone so far as to hire an architect to prepare the plans before he was dissuaded from the scheme. In 1869 the Commodore actually did erect a huge bronze statue of himself on the cornice of the Hudson River Railroad's new freight station at St. John's Park in New York, which he unveiled with bands, a bishop, and New York Mayor A. Oakley Hall in attendance.

Trains of the New York & Harlem began operating from the new Grand Central Depot on October 9, 1871. Through trains of the New York Central & Hudson River began using the terminal on November 13, 1871, although some local trains continued to run from the old Hudson River station at 30th Street and Ninth Avenue. These, too, soon began to operate from Grand Central and only the *Dolly Varden,* a shuttle train from Spuyten Duyvil, continued to operate to and from 30th Street on the West Side for many years. The *Dolly Varden,* as a matter of fact, survived well into the present century, and the 30th Street station lasted until 1931.

The New Haven Railroad, apparently because of a dispute with the Harlem over rental charges for the new depot, continued to operate its trains south through Fourth Avenue by horse power to the old 27th Street station for more than a year after Grand Central was completed. Finally, the necessary arrangements were concluded and the New Haven, too, began using Grand Central on November 21, 1872, after which the old station at 27th Street was converted by showman P.T. Barnum into what later became known as Madison Square Garden, the first of the four New York arenas to bear that name.

From the very beginning, traffic at Grand Central was exceptionally heavy; in its first year the terminal was handling an average of more than 130 train movements daily. Despite this great traffic the train shed was kept remarkably quiet, and free of smoke and gases, by means of some unusual operating procedures.

The ringing of locomotive bells was prohibited, and the use of whistles was allowed only in emergencies. Locomotives for outbound trains stood outside the train shed until just before departure time, when they backed in and coupled on. Locomotives of most inbound trains were kept out of the shed altogether by means of an interesting "flying switch" procedure, which was described thus by Arthur Curran in a *Bulletin* of the Railway & Locomotive Historical Society:

"As soon as these trains emerged from the Park Avenue tunnel, a group of passengers would instantly crowd around the front door of the first car to witness this simple operation. The engine would work hard on the up-grade to 49th Street. At this point the engineer would suddenly shut off steam to relieve the tension on the draft gear. A brakeman would then release the coupler and let out a shout, at the same time waving his right hand. The engineer would then put on as much steam as he could, the air-brake hose would part with a hissing snap and the engine would scurry ahead to the track already mentioned [an extra inbound track]. The towerman, whose business it was to watch these operations, would then throw a switch and the cars would roll, of their own momentum, into the annex."

Brakemen then used the hand brakes to bring the cars to a halt at the platforms.

In addition to keeping smoke and gases out of the train shed, the object of the "flying switch" was also to save time. The locomotives were able to proceed to the engine house immediately for servicing, and the cars were already in place for another trip. Despite the evident dangers of the practice, there apparently was never a serious accident.

In order to avoid a conflict between arriving and departing passengers, Grand Central's designers had placed the outbound tracks on the west side of the train shed, and the inbound tracks on the east side. This, unfortunately, introduced still another operating problem by requiring left-hand operation of trains in the terminal area. Initially, the inbound and outbound tracks crossed over each other at 53rd Street, an extremely awkward location. In 1888, the crossovers were moved north to Spuyten Duyvil and White Plains, and later to Croton Falls, and trains operated left-handed south of those points until the present Grand Central Terminal was built early in this century.

The movement of trains into and out of the depot was controlled by a dispatcher installed in a cabin high on the north wall of the train shed, overlooking the terminal throat. By means of an elaborate system of electric bell signals he was able to control the loading of passengers and baggage in the depot, and the departure of trains. A system of electro-magnetic signals protected train movements in the approaches to the depot.

Long before the Grand Central Depot was built, the tracks of the Harlem, which were laid almost entirely at street level, had constituted an annoyance to the public along Fourth Avenue and its cross streets. The problem only grew worse as the city's population increased and urban development moved steadily northward on Manhattan Island. But with the coming of Grand Central and its traffic of more than a hundred daily trains, the situation became intolerable.

Conditions were particularly bad just north of the station, where the railroad had installed

From the vantage point of his post Grand Central's terminal dispatcher controlled the flow of traffic. The array of buttons on the table controlled a system of electric bells that enabled him to signal various instructions to gatemen, baggagemen, and train crews. The inset shows the electro-magnetically controlled indicator which showed when a block was occupied or clear.—NEW YORK PUBLIC LIBRARY

a huge yard that extended all the way to 49th Street from the north end of the train shed at 45th Street, and west to Madison Avenue. The several street crossings at this location were at grade, and the frequent passage of arriving and departing trains and the almost constant movement of switch engines made any attempt to cross the tracks a risky business. The railroad put up some posts and chains in a rudimentary form of grade crossing protection. This helped somewhat, but not nearly enough.

The Fourth Avenue Improvement scheme, jointly financed by the New York & Harlem and the City of New York and constructed during 1872-4, substantially relieved the problems caused by the great volume of train movements on the grade-level Harlem road north of Grand Central. Drawings in the February 15, 1873 issue of *Frank Leslie's Illustrated Newspaper* depict some of the typical features of the work. This bridge at 45th Street just north of the depot, carried both foot and carriage traffic over the tracks.—PENN CENTRAL COMPANY

Typical scenes of activity at Grand Central Depot were depicted by artist Charles Bunnell in this series of drawings for the July 13, 1889, issue of *Frank Leslie's Illustrated Newspaper.*— NEW YORK PUBLIC LIBRARY

These two drawings from an issue of *Frank Leslie's Illustrated Newspaper* show the interlocking plant and crossover arrangement at 53rd Street which permitted trains to change to or from the system of left-handed running that prevailed in the Grand Central terminal area.—BOTH PENN CENTRAL COMPANY

Soon the Manhattan press had a campaign against the situation going in full cry, frequently with greatly exaggerated reports of injuries and deaths from the trains, although even the truth was none too good. "Every few days there were accounts of the killing and wounding of persons about that frightful network of rails just beyond the depot," wrote a reporter for *Frank Leslie's Illustrated Newspaper* in 1873. "Occasionally, owing to the misplacement of a switch, a locomotive leaped its own pair of rails, rushed away, crashing through buildings, and fetching up in tracts of ground reserved for less destructive objects."

A poet wrote and published an anti-railroad broadside, which urged the sinking of the tracks below ground level. Increasingly, the public demanded just that, and a bill that would compel the railroad to lower its tracks was even introduced in the Legislature at Albany.

Finally, the Vanderbilts gave in and a plan was formulated by Isaac Buckhout, the Harlem's chief engineer, that would provide the road with a grade-separated line, widened to four tracks, all the way to the Harlem River. The Fourth Avenue Improvement Company was formed to carry out the work, and the shrewd Vanderbilt even managed to persuade the city to pay half the cost of the construction.

Placement of the track below grade at the depot itself was considered impractical, and the lowering of the grade was started at 45th Street, with an open cut between retaining walls beginning at 49th Street. Elevated bridges for carriage and foot traffic were built at 45th and 48th streets, with foot bridges provided at the two intermediate streets. Seven more foot bridges were constructed over the open cut from 49th Street to 56th Street.

From 56th to 67th Street the tracks were placed in what was termed a "beam tunnel." This consisted of two single-track side tunnels, connected for ventilation purposes with a double-track center tunnel that was open at the top and spanned with iron beams. This arrangement left a series of ventilation slots or vents in a 50-foot landscaped boulevard strip down the middle of Fourth Avenue. An iron railing surrounded both the vents and the outer borders of the boulevard strip. Fourth

An elevated bridge between 52nd and 53rd streets carried pedestrians above the four-track open cut. (BELOW) North of the 56th Street section of the line the tracks were placed in this partially-covered "beam tunnel" which afforded a sort of continuous series of smoke vents set in a landscaped boulevard.—BOTH PENN CENTRAL COMPANY

North of 115th Street the Fourth Avenue Improvement scheme placed the New York & Harlem line in a four-track open cut that extended all the way through Harlem to the Harlem River. Bridges carried cross streets over the tracks at every block. This drawing shows the Harlem station that was provided at 126th Street.—PENN CENTRAL COMPANY

Avenue, by this time beginning to be known as Park Avenue, was widened to a width of 140 feet, with a 27-foot carriage way and a 15-foot sidewalk on either side of the landscaped boulevard. The overall effect was widely admired, and contributed greatly to the thoroughfare's eventual upgrading into one of the city's most prestigious streets. Still, with the frequency of train movements being what it was, the effect of the vents must have seemed, as architectural historian James M. Finch has put it, "like nothing so much as the fumaroles around an active volcano!"

From 67th to 71st Street the tracks were placed in a full tunnel, constructed of brick, and then in a second "beam tunnel" section that extended north to 80th Street. A second brick tunnel carried the tracks between 80th and 98th streets. The line then crossed the Harlem Flats on an immense stone viaduct between 98th and 115th streets. Beyond 115th, the line was placed in an open cut for the remainder of the distance to the Harlem River, with bridges constructed across the 15-foot-deep cut at each cross street.

Below grade stations were provided at 60th, 73rd, 86th, and 126th streets, while an elevated station was constructed at 110th Street.

Construction for the Fourth Avenue Improvement began in 1872, but it was fully two years before it was completed, and while the engineers struggled to drill and blast their cuts and tunnels through the hard Manhattan rock, the press and public continued their uproar.

This temporary trestle carried trains between 100th and 116th streets during the construction of the Harlem Flats viaduct in 1873. The New York & Harlem train is southbound to Grand Central.—PENN CENTRAL COMPANY

This engraving of the completed Harlem Flats viaduct by artist J. N. Allan dates to about 1875. The 110th Street station is in the foreground, while further south can be seen the entrance to the Park Avenue tunnel at 96th Street.—J. CLARENCE DAVIES COLLECTION, MUSEUM OF THE CITY OF NEW YORK (BELOW) One of the Harlem stations forming a part of the improvement schemes.

Grand Central was considered much too far uptown when it was built, but as the city grew steadily northward on Manhattan, commercial activity and hotels soon followed the depot to the 42nd Street area. By the time this woodcut by artist L. Oram was published around 1885, the handsome Grand Union Hotel was conveniently located across the street from Grand Central. According to the promotional text that accompanied this broadside, the Grand Union offered cuisine and wines of superior merit, an elevator and all improvements, and elegantly furnished rooms, at rates of only a dollar and upwards per day.—J. CLARENCE DAVIES COLLECTION, MUSEUM OF THE CITY OF NEW YORK

The caption that accompanied this 1890's illustration for *Leslie's* assured readers that no unusual urban disturbance was taking place, but only that an inordinate number of New York cabmen were competing for the favor of an arriving passenger at the Grand Central Depot. (BELOW) The fascination of the public with the American West proved a sure-fire circulation builder for the flamboyant publisher of *Frank Leslie's Illustrated Newspaper* when he organized a grand tour of artists, photographers, and writers to describe the glories of the West. The party departed Grand Central Depot on the evening of April 10, 1877, aboard a Wagner palace sleeping car especially redecorated and named *Frank Leslie* for the journey.—BOTH NEW YORK PUBLIC LIBRARY

THE FAST MAIL

Although the original *Fast Mail* installed by William H. Vanderbilt in 1875 lasted but ten months, owing to the failure of Congress to provide sufficient funds for its continuation, a comparable train was reestablished in 1877 and remained a New York Central & Hudson River fixture for many years. This illustration by Herbert Denman from the March 1889 issue of *Scribner's Magazine* depict the urgent pace of postal and railway workers as they prepare for the nightly departure from Grand Central Depot of No. 11, the New York and Chicago Fast Mail. (RIGHT) At Grand Central mail is loaded aboard one of the train's splendid postal cars, which were painted white, with cream tinted borderings and gilt ornamentation; decorated with the U.S. coat-of-arms; and lettered in gilt with the name of a New York Governor or a member of President Garfield's cabinet. (BELOW) Here a fast 4-4-0 American Standard emerges from Grand Central's train shed with the *Fast Mail's* four gleaming white postal cars, Chicago-bound on an urgent schedule that would see the train in its western terminal in an unprecedented time of only 26 hours.—PENN CENTRAL COMPANY

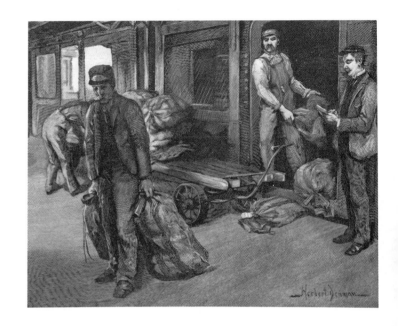

The Commodore's great station was supposed to be good "for all time," but only 15 years later the railroad's traffic had so increased that a major improvement and expansion program became necessary. During 1885-86 the railroad rearranged and enlarged its yard at the depot, and provided it with improved interlocking switches and signals. A new Annex, with a seven-track, 100-foot wide train shed, was constructed on the east side of the original depot. This was used thereafter to receive incoming trains. At Mott Haven, 5 miles north in The Bronx, a new yard was constructed in 1888 for the repair, cleaning, and storage of the Central's trains.

Still another view of the 42nd Street facade dating to around 1890 shows that the openings in the east tower for the passage of horsedrawn cars into Fourth Avenue have been long since closed. The tracks into the Fourth Avenue tunnel where trains of the Harlem and the New Haven roads once passed remain but are now used only by city horse cars.—PENN CENTRAL COMPANY

During 1888-90 another major project was carried out north of the Harlem River, where the line was widened to four tracks, equipped with automatic block signals, and placed below grade for a distance of 5 miles between 138th Street and Woodlawn.

Between 1893 and 1896 still another major improvement to the Grand Central approaches was carried out. From 110th Street to the Harlem River the line that had been placed below grade at such great cost 20 years before was now raised above street level on a great four-track steel viaduct more than a mile in length, and a new high-level, four-track drawbridge, 398 feet long, was built over the Harlem River. The work cost $3 million, half of it paid by the city, and was done largely to permit the conversion of the Harlem River to a ship canal. NYC&HR president Chauncey M. Depew was not happy about it, remarking to a *Harper's Weekly* reporter, "It is not within reason that New York will suffer the inconvenience of having that canal cut the city in two in the middle after a few years more. It will be filled in and built over. It is a mistaken undertaking."

As the end of the century approached, the Central again found itself in need of an

Artist W. Louis Sonntag, Jr. illustrated the new four-track Harlem River drawbridge and the new steel viaduct through Harlem for readers of the May 4, 1895, *Harper's Weekly.*—AUTHOR'S COLLECTION

Chauncey M. Depew, president of the NYC&HR at the time of the Harlem improvements of 1895, didn't think much of the Harlem River ship canal project that obliged the railroad to build an expensive new drawbridge. "It is a mistaken undertaking," he said. An attorney, politician, orator of renowned ability and a protege of Commodore Vanderbilt, Depew served the railroad for 62 years, 14 of them as its president and another 30 as chairman of the board.—AUTHOR'S COLLECTION (BELOW) Only the relocated entrance canopy establishes the period of this Grand Central view at the 42nd Street and Vanderbilt Avenue corner as postdating the 1900 remodeling. By this time electric cars have replaced the horse cars of earlier years.—LIBRARY OF CONGRESS

BIRD'S-EYE VIEW OF THE REMODELLED GRAND CENTRAL STATION, FROM THE BALCONY OF THE MANHATTAN HOTEL

EAST END OF THE GENERAL WAITING-ROOM, SHOWING STAIRWAY TO THE ELEVATED RAILWAY STATION.

THE GENERAL WAITING-ROOM—THE LARGEST IN THE WORLD—LOOKING NORTHEAST.

A CORNER IN THE WOMEN'S ROOM.

This two-page spread of drawings from the February 5, 1898, issue of *Harper's Weekly* depict architect Bradford L. Gilbert's design for the remodeling of Grand Central. The exterior work was executed substantially as shown here, but the interior changes were not. The drawings are by the architect.— LIBRARY OF CONGRESS

The original Bradford Gilbert plans for the 1898 revisions included extensive interior alterations to the terminal's public spaces. This drawing, from the February 19, 1897, issue of *Railroad Gazette*, shows the planned union waiting room, or rotunda, said to be the largest of its kind in the world. The room's design was strikingly similar to that for Gilbert's Illinois Central Station, completed at Chicago a few years before. For reasons now unknown the Gilbert design for the interior work was given up; and when the work was carried out in 1900, Philadelphia architect Samuel Huckel, Jr. was in charge.—LIBRARY OF CONGRESS

expansion of its Manhattan terminal facilities. Population had continued to grow; by 1900 the five boroughs of the newly-united city of Greater New York would have a population of more than 3.4 million. Suburban development now extended well north of the Harlem River into The Bronx and Westchester County, and daily commuters formed an increasingly important share of the railroads' passenger traffic. More than 500 daily trains operated to and from Grand Central. This was more than three times the level of 1871.

Once again, the railroad planned a costly expansion of its terminal facilities. Most of the work this time was concentrated on an extensive enlargement and reconstruction of the terminal building itself. First, the depot building was enlarged by the addition of three stories to provide additional office space. Both the additional stories and the original brick exterior were covered with an imitation stone veneer, made of cement. The result was a rather undistinguished, massive structure in the baroque style, surmounted by four domed clock towers, roofed in copper, which in turn were flanked by carved stone eagles, with wings spread. Although there seems little similarity between the original Grand Central

A view of the French Renaissance waiting room of Grand Central shows its ornate frieze and cornice detail, with panels naming the principal cities served by the terminal's railroads. —LIBRARY OF CONGRESS

Grand Central's interior remodeling of 1900 added this elaborate Vanderbilt Avenue lobby.—LIBRARY OF CONGRESS

Grand Central's Bureau of Information could be reached from the waiting room or the concourse. —PENN CENTRAL COMPANY

of 1869-71 and this reconstruction, close inspection of photographs reveals that the lower floors of the original were indeed incorporated into the latter.

This part of the work, completed in 1898, was carried out under the supervision of Colonel Walter Katté, the railroad's chief engineer. The design was by New York architect Bradford L. Gilbert, whose design for the Illinois Central Station at Chicago a few years earlier had been a much more notable work.

Much more important, from the viewpoint of accommodating the ever-increasing flow of railroad passengers, were the extensive interior revisions to the structure that were completed in 1900. This work was planned and supervised by Philadelphia architect Samuel Huckle, Jr. and William J. Wilgus, who had succeeded Katté as chief engineer of the New York Central & Hudson River the previous year, and its chief purpose was to provide a more efficient internal arrangement of the building's passenger facilities. After nearly thirty years, the depot's separate waiting rooms for each of the three railroads were to be replaced by a single large, combined waiting room. "At last the depot with its yard," wrote Wilgus years later, "was to be used in common by the owner and its two tenants as a union station in the full meaning of the term."

The train shed and its annex were rearranged to provide 11 platforms, served by 19 tracks under cover. At the north end of the train shed a baggage subway and electric lifts were installed, linking the outbound platforms with the inbound baggage room on the east side of the train shed and a new outbound baggage room, which took the place of the former NYC&HR and Harlem waiting rooms on the Vanderbilt Avenue side.

At the south end of the train shed, on the 42nd Street side, the terminal tracks were shortened by 73 feet to provide room for the construction of a large, consolidated waiting room, 179 feet by 70 feet. The room had a ceiling 36 feet high which was covered with arched skylights of leaded glass. Adjacent to the waiting room, in the space formerly occupied by the New Haven's waiting room, were new ticket offices for the three railroads. Between the waiting room and the tracks a

A view from the train shed towards the new Grand Central concourse and waiting room added in 1900 clearly shows how a portion of the original track space under the shed was given over to the construction of the new facilities.—LIBRARY OF CONGRESS (LEFT) This elaborate iron grillwork separated the new concourse from the platforms in the 1900 remodeling. Just beyond the train gates was a narrow baggage runway.— PENN CENTRAL COMPANY

A New Haven 4-4-0 American Standard switches in the Grand Central yard at about 46th Street in this 1899 view. Visible are the Annex train shed added in 1886 (LEFT) and the domed towers of the station building's 1898 enlargement, but the ornate north facade of the train shed remains unchanged since its erection in 1871.—NEW YORK HISTORICAL SOCIETY (BELOW) Grand Central's great iron train shed was kept free of smoke and gases by keeping the locomotives of outbound trains outside the shed until just before departure time. Visible in this view taken just north of the train shed in the late 1800's are two of the ubiquitous 4-4-0 American Standard locomotives that powered the trains of both the New Haven and the New York Central. In the foreground is the pedestrian bridge at 46th Street.—SMITHSONIAN INSTITUTION

large new concourse, with a total area of 12,500 square feet, extended the full width of the train shed. Ornamental iron grilles separated the concourse from the tracks.

The architectural style of the work was described as French Renaissance. The lower portion of the walls of the new rotunda or waiting room was finished in Serra Vozza, Francis Critti, or Breche violet marbles, while floors were of white Italian marble. Woodwork was of mahogany. The ends and sides of the waiting room were divided into arched openings over which there was an ornate frieze and cornice, with panels for the names of 32 principal cities on the lines of the three railroads.

Various other public rooms and facilities were grouped around the waiting room and concourse, and a restaurant was located above the carriage drive and cab stand next to the main entrance on 42nd Street. Stairways and elevators led to the nearby station of the Third Avenue Elevated Railroad in 42nd Street.

Rather revealing of the attitudes of the time was the provision of a new waiting room in the basement for immigrants, "thus entirely relieving," as an account in *The Engineering Record* put it, "the main waiting-room and rotunda of this class of passenger." Immigrants reached their trains by means of a tunnel that ran directly to the concourse. Walls in the immigrant waiting room and passageway were lined with enameled brick, and floored with concrete and asphalt, "the whole capable,"

Another view from the late 1890's shows how the Grand Central terminal yard dominated midtown Manhattan. In the left foreground is the NYC&HR turntable, while beyond is the New Haven's engine terminal. Visible at the right are the Grand Central wreck train and the main switch tower, with the coach storage yard beyond. Looming through the smoke above the 47th Street foot bridge is the station itself.—PENN CENTRAL COMPANY

47

In 1893 the New York Central competed for traffic to the World's Columbian Exposition at Chicago with a splendid new train, the *Exposition Flyer*, which ran between New York and Chicago on an unprecedented 20-hour schedule. Schenectady-built 4-4-0 No. 908 was photographed in the Grand Central Annex on the occasion of the train's first run.—GERALD M. BEST COLLECTION (LEFT) Left-handed running still prevailed in 1899 when NYC&HR G Class 4-4-0 No. 1016 headed south toward Grand Central with a suburban train near 101st Street on the Park Avenue viaduct. Such was the pace of New York's urban growth that the open spaces of scarcely 20 years earlier had already vanished.—PENN CENTRAL COMPANY

LOCOMOTIVES OF
GRAND CENTRAL TERMINAL

Grand Central Depot had its own special motive power for switching the terminal yards. No. 6 was an 0-4-0 built by the Schenectady Locomotive Works in 1884.—ALCO HISTORIC PHOTOS

Two examples of Grand Central motive power of the 1890's are shown in these builder photographs by the Schenectady Locomotive Works. No. 829 was a double-ended 2-6-6 tank engine built in 1891 for the New York Central & Hudson River's increasingly popular suburban services to the Bronx and Westchester County. No. 1 was an 0-6-0 specially designed for Grand Central service by William Buchanan, the railroad's superintendent of motive power and rolling stock, and built by Schenectady in 1896. The engine featured a two-cylinder compound design, a special exhaust reservoir in front of the cylinders, and a variable exhaust in the smokebox, which were said to render the locomotive "practically noiseless."—BOTH ALCO HISTORIC PHOTOS

This engaging picture of Grand Central depicts the new Annex and the close proximity of the El station to the depot complex. (BELOW) In a view southward in Park Avenue from Grand Central of a few years later, automobile traffic has largely replaced the horse-drawn vehicles of the earlier scene above. The once-prestigious Grand Union Hotel at the left, has fallen on seedy times in its last years—it was finally demolished in 1914—while the new Belmont Hotel at the right, erected by financier August Belmont II in 1908, has taken its place in the affections of Grand Central passengers.—PENN CENTRAL COMPANY

A view north to Grand Central from Park Avenue in 1907 provides an interesting contrast to earlier views. Electric street cars, powered from a conduit system under the street, have replaced the horse cars of the earlier view, and the remodeled Grand Central Station of 1898-1900 has taken the place of the original Vanderbilt structure, but the horsedrawn cabs remained an unchanging part of the urban scene despite the passage of years.—PENN CENTRAL COMPANY

reported the *Record,* "of being cleaned out regularly with a hose."

The capacity of the rebuilt station was given as 10 million passengers annually.

There were improvements to the yard, too, most notably to Grand Central's signal and interlocking systems. One of these changes was the installation of a new pneumatic switch system, which was intended to permit the elimination of the "flying switch" procedure that had been in use for years. When it was first tried out, the new system proved to be something of a disaster. Trains were delayed in the station or on its approaches for as much as two hours, and after three days the railroad returned temporarily to the use of the

"flying switch." In any event, no amount of tinkering with switches and signals could solve the real problem in the approaches to Grand Central, which was that there simply wasn't enough track space to effectively handle all of the traffic.

Along with the thoroughgoing 1898-1900 changes, the terminal by this time had been renamed the Grand Central Station. But despite all the improvements, and new name or not, Commodore Vanderbilt's splendid old palace on 42nd Street simply was no longer equal to the demands of its traffic or the pressures of a growing city. Because of this, Grand Central Station was to have a very short life indeed.

From 1878 until its closing in 1923 the short stub off the Third Avenue El that ended at the Grand Central Station shown in this January 1907 photograph was a conspicuous 42nd Street landmark. A marble staircase from Grand Central's main waiting room afforded direct access to the El platforms.—PENN CENTRAL COMPANY

3

An Engineer and His Grand Design

Despite the extensive improvements of 1898-1900, the inadequacies of the old Grand Central were becoming more evident all the time as traffic continued to grow. Yard space at the terminal, still confined to essentially the same real estate that had been available in 1869, was insufficient to meet the needs of a traffic that by 1900 averaged more than 500 daily trains, exclusive of switching movements. The lack of switching leads and the frequent inability to clear the ladder tracks rapidly enough often required that incoming trains be held in the Park Avenue tunnel. And finally, the city was growing increasingly restive toward the barrier to cross-town traffic created by the surface-level station and yard tracks from 42nd to 56th Street, a distance of three-quarters of a mile.

A sizable expansion of the existing terminal to relieve these congestion problems seemed hardly to be a feasible solution, for Grand Central was set down in the midst of what by this time had become some of the world's most expensive real estate.

The inadequacies of the railroad's terminal facilities were further compounded by a severe shortage of office spaces. During the 1890's architect Bradford L. Gilbert had been retained for the design of an 11-story railroad office building on the southwest corner of 42nd Street and Park Avenue. This was never built, and the three stories of office space added to the old station in the 1898 rebuilding were insufficient to meet the needs. Soon afterward the railroad was considering a plan to erect a new office building in place of the old Annex.

The New York Central suffered from the effects of another serious New York terminal problem as well, and the solution to this second problem was to prove the key to that of the first.

Smoke and cinders from the locomotives of the hundreds of daily train movements had become an intolerable nuisance for Manhattan

residents along the railroad's tracks. Even more critical were the operating problems that steam locomotives created in the 2 miles of tunnel or partially-covered cut along Park Avenue that carried trains into Grand Central. Frequently the tracks here were so heavily choked with smoke and steam that it became impossible to read signals, a condition which contributed to several serious accidents. A particularly severe collision occurred on the morning of January 8, 1902, when an inbound New York Central train ran past a red signal in the Park Avenue cut at 54th Street and crashed into the rear car of a halted New Haven train, killing 15 commuters. The public outcry that followed this mishap was instrumental in an action by the New York Legislature the following year which prohibited the operation of steam locomotives south of the Harlem River after July 1, 1908.

The solution to the New York Central's difficult New York terminal problems would require a project of extraordinary magnitude, and it would engage the talents of a number of exceptionally capable men. But the basic concept for the brilliant solution was the work of just one man, William J. Wilgus, the New York Central and Hudson River's chief engineer and a civil engineer of remarkable ability and accomplishment.

Dating from November 19, 1906, this view of the approaches to Grand Central Station and the adjoining yards gives a good idea of the magnitude of the New York Central's smoke and congestion problems at its New York terminal. Third rail was already in place in much of the terminal area, but regular operation of electric trains did not begin until a month later.—PENN CENTRAL COMPANY

William J. Wilgus, vice-president and chief engineer of the New York Central & Hudson River RR, was an engineer of exceptional ability who supervised a far-reaching rebuilding of the railroad at the turn of the century.—DONALD DUKE COLLECTION

Like a number of his contemporaries in 19th century and early 20th century engineering, Wilgus was a largely self-made engineer who doubtless would have failed to reach his high position in today's degree-conscious professional world. Born at Buffalo, New York, on November 20, 1865, Wilgus graduated from Buffalo Central High School in 1883, and then studied for the next two years under Marsden Davey, a Buffalo civil engineer. His formal education ended at the age of 20 with the completion of a Cornell University correspondence course in drafting.

In 1885 Wilgus took a post as a surveyor and draftsman with the Minnesota & Northwestern Railroad, a predecessor line of the Chicago Great Western. By 1890 he had worked his way up through a series of engineering positions to that of division engineer, and had been in charge of the construction of extensive terminals at Minneapolis and East Minneapolis, Minnesota, and at St. Joseph and Kansas City, Missouri. In 1890 he supervised construction of the railroad's extension from St. Joseph to Leavenworth, Kansas. Later that same year Wilgus was appointed locating engineer for the Duluth & Winnipeg Railroad and during 1891-92 he was in charge of construction of the Chicago Union Transfer Railway. In 1892 Wilgus surveyed the extension of the Duluth & Iron Range Rail Road westward from Embarrass Lake to the Mesabi Range.

Still only 28 years old, Wilgus returned east in 1893 to begin a rapid rise through the engineering ranks of the Vanderbilts' New York Central & Hudson River, beginning as an assistant engineer on the Rome, Watertown & Ogdensburg Division. In 1895 he was appointed chief engineer in charge of the construction of the Terminal Railway of Buffalo, and then, in 1897, went to New York City as a resident engineer and then chief assistant engineer for the railroad. Becoming engineer of maintenance of way for the NYC&HR in 1898, Wilgus was responsible for an extensive rehabilitation of the entire system to accommodate heavier motive power. He was named chief engineer in 1899.

Even while he was supervising the extensive revisions to the old Grand Central in 1900, Wilgus had already begun to turn his attention to the need for a still greater augmentation of the railroad's New York terminal facilities. Although the full development of his concept for an entirely new Grand Central Terminal was still several years in the future, it was to evolve through a series of refinements and modifications from ideas developed by Wilgus in 1899.

The key to the solution of the New York Central's terminal problems was found in the new field of electric traction, which had come of age scarcely a decade before with Frank J. Sprague's successful electrification of the Richmond (Virginia) Union Passenger Railway in 1888. By the end of the century electric street railways had grown into a major industry, with a traffic that was rapidly approaching a level of 5 million passengers annually, and the steam-operated elevated railways in both New York and Chicago had begun a conversion to electric operation. But save for a 4-mile electrification of the Baltimore & Ohio Railroad's Howard Street tunnel at Baltimore in 1895, nowhere in the U.S. had electric traction yet been successfully applied to the movement of heavy main line railroad traffic.

In 1899 Wilgus was visited by electric traction pioneer Frank Sprague, who since his notable 1888 electrification of the Richmond street railway system had successfully developed a control system for electric elevators and the "multiple unit" control system for electric trains, which permitted an entire train of electric cars to be controlled as a unit from a single master controller. In the meeting with Wilgus, Sprague proposed the electrification of the Central's Yonkers branch. Wilgus was an enthusiastic listener, and from this conference grew some of the basic elements of the plan eventually adopted for the development of the new Grand Central.

Inspired by Sprague's enthusiasm for electrification, Wilgus completed a plan in June 1899 which proposed the electric operation of suburban trains in the two outside tunnels along Park Avenue, and then by means of new tracks constructed in a widened open cut in Park Avenue south of 56th Street to a loop station to be built beneath the old Grand Central Station and the adjoining land and streets. Thus it was this Wilgus plan of 1899 that introduced the idea of a multi-level terminal to provide additional capacity without a substantial enlargement of the terminal site. By eliminating the problems of ventilation of the smoke and gasses from steam locomotives, electrification, of course, would make the concept practical.

The Wilgus plan was adopted by the Central's board of directors, but construction was never authorized, and the plan was set aside for the next several years. Meanwhile, the public demand for some improvement to the problems caused by the Central's terminal conditions became increasingly urgent. There were proposals that some sort of ventilating apparatus with high chimneys should be installed to relieve the smoke problems, that the Park Avenue tunnel be converted to an open cut, or that compressed air replace steam power for the movement of trains. To solve the terminal congestion problem, for example, an article in the December 1, 1900, issue of *Scientific American* suggested that local traffic be separated from through traffic. Through trains would continue to use the old terminal, proposed the magazine, while local trains would run up an incline from the tunnel entrance to reach a new elevated terminal above the terminal yard. Trains would unload at platforms along a series of concentric loop tracks, and the reload and depart down a second incline.

The public outcry that followed the serious January 1902 accident in the Park Avenue cut brought a new urgency to the Central's consideration of a solution to the terminal problems. Only a few weeks after the accident, the railroad presented the 1899 Wilgus plan to

The original Wilgus plan of 1899, which retained use of the existing Grand Central Station and its surface-level terminal tracks, is depicted by this drawing from the January 31, 1902, *Railroad Gazette.* Beginning at 56th Street, tunnels would descend below grade on either side of the existing tracks to form a below-ground loop beneath the old station and terminal yard. Electrified suburban and through trains would use the loop, which was to have platforms linked with the waiting room in the old station, a new suburban station on the west side of Vanderbilt Avenue between 43rd and 44th streets, and the IRT subway platforms. Steam-powered trains would continue to use the surface level tracks.—DONALD DUKE COLLECTION

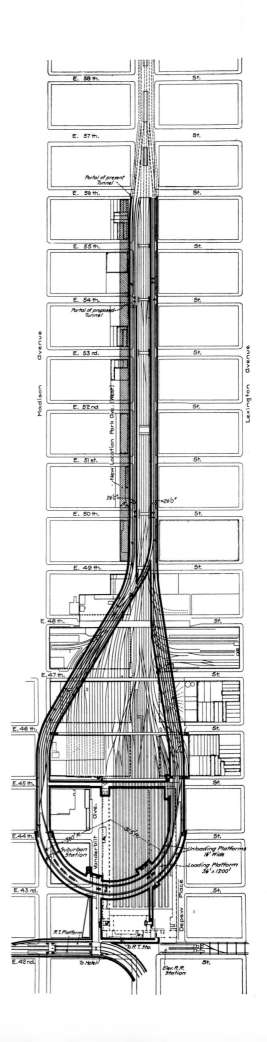

the New York State Board of Railroad Commissioners as a means of increasing terminal capacity and minimizing the smoke problems. In August of the previous year, too, Wilgus had engaged Bion J. Arnold, a noted electrical engineer, to study the practicality of operating the railroad's heavy through traffic with electric power between Grand Central and Mott Haven, just north of the Harlem River crossing. Arnold's report, completed in February 1902, recommended the electrification.

By the end of 1902 the New York Central was firmly committed to an electrification project for its New York terminal operations. A special Electric Traction Commission was established on December 17, 1902, to plan the general features of the project. Wilgus, who was named as New York Central vice president in February 1902, served as chairman of the commission. Consultant members included both Sprague and Arnold, as well as a third distinguished electrical engineer, George Gibbs, who had previously carried out several important electrification projects as chief engineer for the Westinghouse Companies in Europe, and later was to serve as chief engineer for the Pennsylvania Railroad's New York terminal electrification and station construction. A fifth member of the commission was Arthur M. Waitt, the Central's superintendent of motive power, who shortly afterward was replaced in both positions by John F. Deems. Edwin B. Katté, the railroad's electrical engineer, acted as secretary to the commission, and was in direct charge of the electrification work.

The electrification project developed by the Central's Electric Traction Commission went far beyond the immediate requirement for electrification of trackage in Grand Central and its Manhattan approaches. Both through and suburban services were included, and electrification was installed throughout the length of the Central's two principal suburban routes, which extended a distance of some 34 miles along the Hudson River to Croton, and northward on the old Harlem line to North White Plains, 24 miles from Grand Central. The project required an initial fleet of 180 new multiple unit electric suburban cars and 35 95-ton electric locomotives. So great were the power requirements of the electrification that

the utility companies could not supply it, and the New York Central was obliged to build two huge power plants of its own. It was by far the most ambitious railroad electrification yet undertaken in North America and it was clearly, as *Scientific American* termed it, the application of electric traction "on a vast and sweeping scale."

Initial orders for locomotives, substations, and other equipment were placed in the fall of 1903, and a prototype electric locomotive began tests only a year later. The first multiple unit suburban trains began running in December 1906, followed by locomotive-hauled through trains two months later. Initially, electric operation extended only from Grand Central to High Bridge on the Hudson Division and Wakefield on the Harlem Division, and electric operation did not reach its planned terminals at North White Plains and Croton until 1910 and 1913, respectively.

By eliminating the problem of ventilating locomotive gasses, of course, electrification made possible a two-level terminal along the lines first proposed by the 1899 Wilgus plan, thus giving the railroad the substantial expansion of terminal facilities it needed without the prohibitive cost of the additional real estate that would otherwise have been required.

Planning for the new terminal facilities went ahead under Wilgus' direction simultaneously with that for the electrification work. Initial studies for the project were based upon retention of the existing Grand Central Station. The 1899 Wilgus plan had proposed an electrified below-ground loop beneath the existing station and yard. Another Wilgus plan, advanced in December 1902, provided for the placement of two levels of terminal tracks below the existing street level but retained the use of the old station.

But as he considered various schemes for retaining the old station in the project, Wilgus became convinced that this was a far from ideal solution. "In particular," he wrote years later, "it was evident ... that a lofty new building for badly needed additional railroad offices on the site of the Annex would be in unhappy contrast with the neighboring imitation stone depot of less stately height. Why not," he questioned, "tear down the old

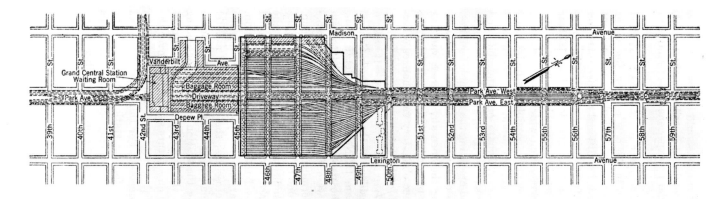

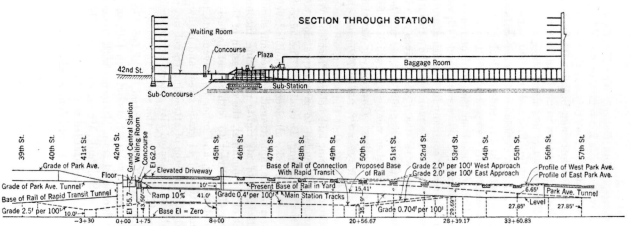

FIG. 8.—PROPOSED TRANSFORMATION AS OF DECEMBER 22, 1902, PREDICATED ON THE UTILIZATION OF AIR RIGHTS

building and train shed and in their place, and in the yard on the north, create a double-level, under-surface terminal on which to super-impose office quarters and revenue producing structures made possible by the intended use of electric motive power?"

As part of this new scheme Wilgus proposed the erection of an adjoining hotel on a vacant block owned by the New York & Harlem between Vanderbilt and Madison avenues and 43rd and 44th streets, and the incorporation of a realty company for acquiring land and operating the rentable facilities.

"The keynote in this plan," wrote Wilgus, "was the utilization of air rights that hitherto were unenjoyable with steam locomotives requiring the open air, or great vaulting spaces, for the dissipation of their products of combustion. Thus from the air would be taken wealth with which to finance obligatory vast changes otherwise nonproductive. Obviously it was the thing to do."

By March 1903 Wilgus had laid before New York Central president William H. Newman a plan which incorporated all of the essential

These drawings, which date from December 22, 1902, show a later Wilgus concept for the Grand Central improvements which still retained the existing station and trainshed. Provision was made for a connection of the suburban level tracks to the IRT subway under lower Park Avenue, but the suburban level loop was apparently not included in this version of the plan.—FROM PAPER NO. 2119, "THE GRAND CENTRAL TERMINAL IN PERSPECTIVE," BY WILLIAM J. WILGUS, TRANSACTIONS OF THE AMERICAN SOCIETY OF CIVIL ENGINEERS, V. 106, 1941.

These two drawings from the January 17, 1903, issue of *Scientific American* show some of the features of the 1902 Wilgus plan, which contemplated retention of the Grand Central Station. In this cutaway drawing (LEFT) is shown the manner in which the proposed connection would be made between the Central's suburban level tracks and the new IRT subway then under construction below Park Avenue. In the scene below, a view looking south toward the trainshed, showing the planned depression of the terminal tracks and the new viaducts above them for Park Avenue and the restored crosstown streets. Park Avenue was to be extended right through the trainshed, and an elevated plaza or driveway for carriages was to be built within the shed for the convenience of arriving or departing passengers.—LIBRARY OF CONGRESS

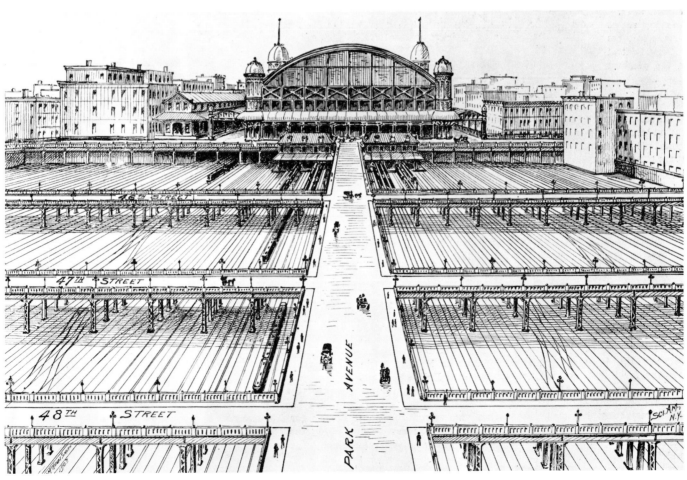

elements of the new Grand Central Terminal as it would finally be realized a decade later. It was to be a 57-track, all-electric, double-level terminal. The lower level was to be provided with a loop to permit the turning of suburban trains, and provision was made in the plans for a connection of these suburban level tracks to the Interborough Rapid Transit subway then being constructed under Park Avenue south of 42nd street, should this become desirable at a later date. An entirely new terminal and office building would replace the old Grand Central Station, and hotels and other revenue-producing structures would be constructed on "air rights" above the terminal tracks. Depression of the tracks below grade level would permit the restoration of the crosstown streets from 45th to 55th Street, and an elevated north-south roadway, circumscribing the terminal building and bridging over 42nd Street, would link upper and lower Park Avenue. One feature of the plan that was never fully realized was a proposal for a broad "Court of Honor" or "Grand Central Park" linked to this north-south roadway and constructed above Park Avenue on a future second level over the intersecting cross streets between 45th and 48th streets.

Cost estimates developed by Wilgus in May 1903 placed the total cost of the New York Central's New York terminal improvements, including the station, yard, electrification, track improvements, and the construction of revenue-producing facilities, at more that $43 million. But, estimated Wilgus, the annual rentals and other income from the project's revenue-producing features would produce an annual return of more than 3 percent on the entire cost of the project, without even considering the benefits gained from operating economies or increased traffic on the greatly improved suburban service.

This drawing, dating from July 1903, shows the evolution of the Wilgus plan for the Grand Central improvements at the time it was approved by the city and work was started. By this time the suburban level loop had been added, but many other changes were still ahead.—COLLECTION OF HERBERT H. HARWOOD

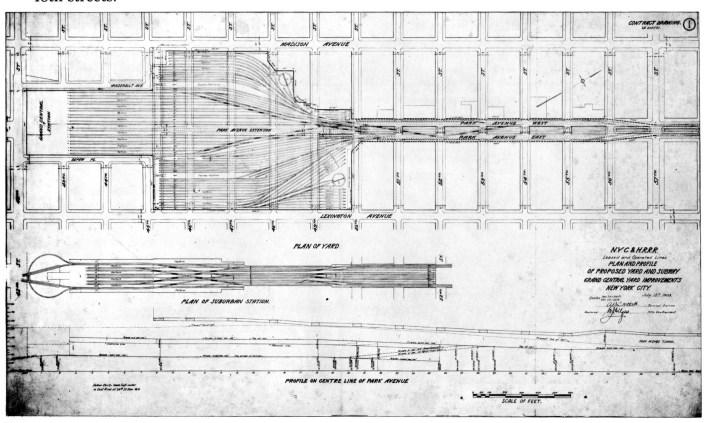

The New York Central had ample reason for celebration on September 30, 1906, when electric motor No. 3405 pulled the first electric train out of the old Grand Central Station.—COLLECTION OF HERBERT H. HARWOOD, JR. (BELOW) This snow scene is evidently from the first few years of electric operation, for steam power still shared Grand Central duties with the new electric motors. Visible in the background are the ornate towers of the 1898 Grand Central Station.—MUSEUM OF THE CITY OF NEW YORK

The New York Central's plans were presented to a special committee of New York City's Board of Estimate and Apportionment on June 3, 1903. Commented Nelson P. Lewis, chief engineer to the board, "The plans impress me as providing perhaps the finest railway terminal station in the world . . . I am deeply impressed with the magnanimous spirit of the company in planning things in a large and comprehensive way, without regard to cost."

The city's formal approval of the work, required under state legislation adopted earlier in 1903, was granted on June 19, with July 1, 1903, fixed as the date of commencement of the work. Construction actually began on July 18 with some work on track changes at 47th Street, and the excavation contractor for the terminal site was at work in earnest within another month. Over the next several years there would be many changes in the details of the plans, but the basic outline for the new Grand Central Terminal was now firmly fixed, and it bore the indelible imprint of William J. Wilgus.

The final evolution of Grand Central's exterior design was depicted in this splendid pencil rendering by artist Vernon Howe Bailey for the March 1913 issue of *Architecture*. Just beyond the terminal to the left is shown the planned Biltmore Hotel. The vacant lot to the right, fronting on 42nd Street, was to become the site of the Commodore Hotel.—New York Public Library

4

The Architects and Their Magnificent Structure

Once Wilgus had established the basic concept for the terminal, the railroad turned to the task of selecting an architect for the great new terminal building itself. Early in 1903 competitive design proposals for the project were solicited from four architectural firms. Two of them were among the most distinguished firms of their time. New York's McKim, Mead & White had produced such notable designs as that for the second Madison Square Garden and the Boston Public Library, and had designed many of the buildings for the 1893 World's Columbian Exhibition. Chicago's Daniel H. Burnham had designed New York's Flatiron Building, had been the chief architect for the Columbian Exhibition, and had just been commissioned to design the Washington Union Station. Less well known were Samuel Huckel, Jr. of Philadelphia, who had worked with Wilgus on the interior renovation of the old Grand Central Station carried out in 1900, and the architectural partnership of Charles A. Reed and Allen H. Stem of St. Paul, Minnesota.

Stanford White, of McKim, Mead & White, submitted a design which featured a great 700-foot office tower, from the top of which he proposed a 300-foot jet of steam which would be illuminated at night by red lights to serve as both a beacon to ships at sea and an advertisement for the railroad. Samuel Huckle proposed an ornate, multi-turreted office building above the terminal, with a hotel wing extending to Madison Avenue between 43rd and 44th streets. No drawings of the Burnham proposal seem to have survived.

Surprisingly, perhaps, the choice went not to one of the widely known competitors, but to the relatively unknown Reed & Stem firm. But if it was not well known to the general public, the firm had a well-established reputation within the railroad industry. Charles Reed himself, who largely developed the Grand Central design, had previously designed terminals for no less than five different railroad companies, and by the time the partnership was terminated by Reed's death in 1911, the firm had designed some-

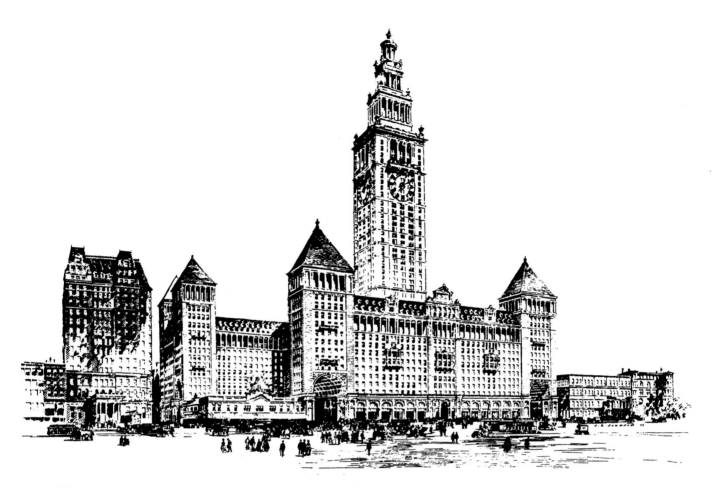

Architect Stanford White developed this many-towered design for the new Grand Central Terminal in the 1903 competition. Park Avenue traffic would have passed through the arched passages in the towers at either side. An illuminated plume of steam from the 700-foot clock tower at the center would have made the terminal an extraordinary Manhattan sight.—DONALD O. EISELE COLLECTION (LEFT) Although this design for the terminal building submitted by Charles Reed in the 1903 competition bore no resemblance to what was finally built, the "circumferential driveway" and its bridge over 42nd Street were built almost exactly as shown here, and this original Reed design incorporated some of Grand Central's most innovative interior features.—NEW YORK PUBLIC LIBRARY

These two drawings depict the heavily commercial terminal design proposed by Philadelphia architect Samuel Huckel, Jr. Shown in the view from about 50th Street and Lexington Avenue are the viaducts that were planned to carry the crosstown streets and Park Avenue across the below-grade terminal tracks, and the manner in which the Park Avenue extension would have passed through the terminal building. The view from the Madison Avenue side (BELOW) shows the hotel wing Huckel would have placed on the site that was eventually occupied by the Biltmore Hotel. The large opening at its center evidently would have provided a Madison Avenue link with the Park Avenue extension within the terminal building.—NEW YORK PUBLIC LIBRARY

thing like 100 railroad stations.

The Reed & Stem firm was well known, too, to the New York Central & Hudson River. At the time of the Grand Central competition the firm was already working with Wilgus on the design of the railroad's new station at Troy, New York, and Wilgus, as a point of interest, had married Charles Reed's sister, May, in 1892.

There were those who suggested that the firm was selected because of this familial connection between Wilgus and Reed. This may well have been so, but there can be no doubt that Charles Reed produced an architectural concept for the terminal building that matched and complemented the vision of Wilgus' overall plan in an extraordinarily successful way.

A part of the Wilgus plan that presented a particularly difficult problem was the engineer's requirement that the design provide for the continuation of Park Avenue through the

site of the new terminal building. Other architects in the competition satisfied the requirement with designs in which the terminal building straddled the Park Avenue extension. But Reed proposed the idea of an elevated "circumferential plaza," which wrapped the traffic lanes of the extension around the outside of the building, preserving the unity of its interior spaces. It was Reed, too, who proposed the concept of the elevated "Court of Honor" above Park Avenue to the north of the terminal. Both of these features developed by Reed were incorporated into the plan Wilgus put forth to NYC&HR president Newman in late March 1903, and subsequently presented for the approval of the City of New York.

Another difficult problem that was handled extremely well in the Reed & Stem design was that of moving Grand Central's great crowds easily and smoothly between street level and the terminal's two below-ground concourses.

Monumental public buildings faced the elevated Park Avenue "Court of Honor" proposed by architect Charles Reed in his 1903 design submittal for the Grand Central project. This rendering of the Reed plan faces south from 48th Street toward the terminal and its high office tower.—NEW YORK PUBLIC LIBRARY

French-trained architect and artist Whitney Warren was largely responsible for the great architectural distinction of the Grand Central design. His architectural partnership with Charles Wetmore was eminently successful, including among its later accomplishments such New York hotels as the Biltmore, the Ambassador, and the Ritz-Carlton, as well as a number of railroad terminals and buildings.—NEW YORK PUBLIC LIBRARY

To do this, the architects designed a brilliant system of broad, gently sloping ramps that proved to work exceptionally well. Nothing quite like it had ever been done before.

And, finally, Charles Reed conceived the idea of the lofty, splendid room that was Grand Central's main concourse, which remains to this day perhaps New York's finest interior space.

Although it got off to a good beginning, the architectural work for the Grand Central project was to prove the source of extraordinary controversy. Soon after Reed & Stem had won the design competition and prepared the initial drawings for the city's approval, they were persuaded to associate for the project with the New York architectural firm of Warren & Wetmore. Just why this was done was never completely made known, although there was the fairly clear implication that it was another matter of familial connections. For Whitney Warren, the senior member of the new firm, was both a cousin and a close friend of William K. Vanderbilt, the Commodore's grandson and then chairman of the board of the New York Central & Hudson River.

Whatever the reasons for the addition of the second firm, Whitney Warren brought an impressive talent to the Grand Central project. Born at New York in 1864, he studied briefly at Columbia University and then at the École des Beaux-Arts in Paris under Daumet and Girault from 1885 to 1894. Returning to the U.S., he began his practice of architecture in the New York office of McKim,

Mead & White, but left several years later, forming his own partnership with Charles D. Wetmore in 1898. Wetmore, a Harvard-trained lawyer, had engaged Warren to design a country home for him. Much impressed with his client's own architectural skill, Warren persuaded him to give up the practice of law and join him in the field of architecture, which Wetmore promptly did. The partners gained early recognition when they won a design competition for a new clubhouse for the New York Yacht Club and subsequently developed an extremely successful practice, specializing in railroad architecture, hotels, business buildings, and residences.

Although Charles Reed was named executive head of the Associated Architects, as the new arrangement was called, his original design concept was largely discarded in favor of a much more monumental concept advanced by Whitney Warren. Two of the most notable features of the original Reed design, the elevated driveway encircling the terminal building and bridging 42nd Street and the elevated Park Avenue "Court of Honor," were eliminated. Charles Reed's original plan for the construction of a high office building above the terminal on 42nd Street was also discarded, stairways replaced Reed's system of ramps, and the treatment of the waiting room and concourse areas was substantially altered.

As the construction work went forward there were a number of alterations to the terminal plans, but the basic concepts of the

A cutaway view was always a popular way to show the inner workings of Grand Central's complex design. One of the earliest is this drawing by artist F. Cresson Schell from the February 4, 1905, issue of *Harper's Weekly*, which was based on the Whitney Warren design that supplanted the original architectural scheme developed by Charles Reed in 1903. Shown here are (A) ticket lobby, (B) express level concourse, (C) waiting room, (D) suburban level concourse, (E) restaurant, (F) suburban level loop, and (G) track connection to the IRT subway. Absent from this version of the design were the broad ramps between the terminal's different levels that had been proposed by the original Reed design.—AUTHOR'S COLLECTION

These three drawings show how the Whitney Warren design for Grand Central evolved through several variations. The drawing from the December 9, 1905, *Scientific American Supplement* (LEFT) shows the original version, which incorporated intersecting ceiling vaults in a cruciform pattern for its spectacular main concourse. By the time artist Vernon Howe Bailey did this rendering for the January 12, 1907, *Harper's Weekly* (BELOW), the design had taken on much of the character of the building that was finally built. — AUTHOR'S COLLECTION

Warren & Wetmore revisions remained a part of the project until 1909, when the plans were once again substantially revised. According to some accounts at least, these changes were made at the insistence of the New Haven Railroad, which had a strong voice in matters concerning the terminal under the terms of its agreements with the Harlem road. In any event, this third plan reincorporated, on an expanded scale, all of the basic features of the original Charles Reed design. Back in were the elevated roadway around the terminal and the interior ramps, and provision was made for the later addition of the Park Avenue "Court of Honor." Provision was also made for the later construction of a high rise office building above the terminal concourse, essentially along the lines originally proposed by Reed in 1903.

Another sort of architectural controversy broke out in November 1911 on the death of Charles Reed. It was alleged later that Whitney Warren, even on the way back to New York from Reed's funeral at Scarsdale, began a move to take over the entire project

In a slightly later version of the Warren design drawn by artist H. M. Pettit, the statuary group and clock on the 42nd Street facade have assumed substantially their final form. Charles Reed's novel elevated circumferential roadway and bridge across 42nd Street were not restored to the design until 1909.—MUSEUM OF THE CITY OF NEW YORK

The final design for the terminal adopted in 1909, which incorporated the best features of both the Charles Reed and Whitney Warren designs, is shown in this drawing by artist Jules Guerin for the December 7, 1912, issue of *Scientific American.* —AUTHOR'S COLLECTION

for the Warren & Wetmore firm. Warren was successful in this attempt and the railroad's contract with Associated Architects was abrogated and replaced by a new contract with Warren & Wetmore as the architects in charge of Grand Central for the remainder of the work. When the project was finally completed in 1913, it was Whitney Warren alone who was generally credited as its architect.

In addition to the manner in which the breach of the architectural partnership unfairly deprived Reed & Stem of credit for its work, there was disagreement over the distribution of the architectural fees. Subsequently, Allen Stem took the matter to court, and when the case was finally settled in 1921 Warren & Wetmore was obliged to hand over a settlement of more than $400,000 to Stem and the Reed estate.

It is not easy to establish with any certainty the specific contributions of each of the principal architects to the final design of the terminal. Clearly, Charles Reed may be credited with the conception of Grand Central's innovative functional features. And just as clearly, at least a large share of the credit for the details and refinement of the terminal's architectural treatment must go to the flamboyant and artistically brilliant Beaux Arts scholar, Whitney Warren.

There can be no question that the architectural association that produced the design for Grand Central Terminal was a frequently unhappy and discordant relationship between two brilliant, strong-willed men, each with his own firmly held convictions about the kind of structure that should be built. Yet it seems evident, too, that the final product of all this conflict was a design for the Grand Central Terminal that was much superior to what either of them would have accomplished alone. For what they had wrought was, as architectural historian Carroll L. V. Meeks was to call it almost a half century later, "... one of the outstandingly successful stations of history."

It was indeed a magnificent structure. The exterior was designed in what is generally described as "Beaux Arts Eclectic" and was executed in Stony Creek granite and Bedford limestone. The building's principal facade on

These two exterior views of the terminal building are from the April 1913 issue of *Architecture & Building*. The cab exit (ABOVE) was at 45th Street and Park Avenue. The view of the Lexington Avenue side (BELOW) is from the future site of the Commodore Hotel.—BOTH LIBRARY OF CONGRESS

42nd Street was set off by three great arched windows, 33 feet wide and 60 feet high, flanked by Doric columns, and with a huge mythological statuary group by the French sculptor Jules-Alexis Coutan as its central feature. Its significance was explained thus by Whitney Warren:

"The architectural composition consists of three great portals crowned by a sculptural group, the whole to stand as a monument to the glory of commerce as typified by Mercury, supported by moral and mental energy—Hercules and Minerva. All to attest that this great enterprise has grown and exists not merely from the wealth expended, nor by the revenue derived, but by the brain and brawn constantly concentrated upon its development for nearly a century."

The statuary group featured a central figure of Mercury, flanked by figures of Hercules and Minerva, surmounting a huge clock 13 feet in diameter. Carved from Bedford limestone, the group was 60 feet wide, stood 50 feet high, and weighed 1,500 tons. If Grand Central's facade was not to be universally acclaimed by architectural critics, at least no one was ever going to mistake it for something else.

Sculptor Jules Coutan's huge mythological statuary group on Grand Central's 42nd Street facade was clearly one of the terminal's most prominent and distinctive features, but not everyone admired it. Elmer Davis snidely referred to it as "Kolossal," and architectural historian Talbot F. Hamlin termed it "vulgar grandiose."—PENN CENTRAL COMPANY (BELOW) Grand Central's 42nd Street facade still gleamed in its newness when this photograph was taken from Park Avenue around 1914. The circumferential driveway around the building and the bridge across 42nd Street to lower Park Avenue would not be complete for several more years.—LIBRARY OF CONGRESS

The terminal's Modern French interior was much more generally admired, and the lofty main concourse was clearly its dominant feature. The huge room was 275 feet long and 120 feet wide, and its vaulted ceiling rose to a height of 125 feet. The concourse was illuminated by three great arched windows, nearly 60 feet high, at each end, facing Depew Place and Vanderbilt Avenue, and by five graceful clerestory lunettes set in the curve of the vaulted ceiling on each side. Huge bronze chandeliers in galleries on the north and south sides of the concourse, and indirect lighting fixtures around the base of the vaulted ceiling, provided illumination at night. The floor was paved with Tennessee marble, and the walls were covered with a manufactured imitation of the warm, buff-colored Caen stone quarried in Normandy, with wainscots and trimmings of cocoa-colored Botticino marble. A circular information booth, surmounted by a four-faced golden clock, was set down in the very center of the concourse.

By far the most notable feature of the great concourse, though, was the great astronomical mural painted in gold on cerulean blue tempera on the vaulted ceiling from a design by the French painter Paul Helleu. The

Another version of the popular Grand Central cutaway view was this drawing from the December 7, 1912, *Scientific American*, which depicts the terminal's interior facing eastward from a point on Vanderbilt Avenue. Clearly shown are the broad ramps between the terminal's several levels that were one of the designs most notable features.—AUTHOR'S COLLECTION

A classic view of Grand Central's main concourse is provided by this drawing from an early New York Central brochure. The work evidently predates the architect's decision to paint an astronomical mural on the ceiling, for the spectacular design is noticably absent from this rendering.—AUTHOR'S COLLECTION (BELOW) Still new and unstained by age and traffic, Grand Central's main concourse was surely, as architectural historian H.R. Hitchcock termed it, "one of the grandest spaces the early twentieth century ever enclosed." MUSEUM OF THE CITY OF NEW YORK

design, which depicted a Mediterranean winter sky, included some 2,500 stars. The 60 largest stars, which marked the constellations, were illuminated from behind with an adjustable lighting system that gave them the correct celestial magnitude.

Soon after the terminal opened, it was noted that the section of the zodiac depicted by the mural was backwards, and for several decades lively controversy raged over why this was so. It was said, variously, that the placement had been reversed because the constellations looked better that way, that the constellations had been reversed to make them fit the ceiling, or that the thing was only meant to be decorative anyway. The most likely explanation, though, was that Helleu had taken his inspiration from a manuscript of the Medeival period, when it was the convention to depict the heavens as they would be seen from outside the celestial sphere.

Grand Central's "... great blue vault, dotted with stars and lined in dull gold with the figures of the constellations," wrote Talbot Hamlin in his *American Spirit in Architecture*, "seems almost an attempt to make it all part of outdoors." An adjustable lighting system illuminated the 60 largest stars of the constellations at their correct celestial magnitude.—ED NOWAK, PENN CENTRAL COMPANY

The mood of Grand Central's great room on a busy day was captured by artist Louis Ruyl in this pencil drawing for the January 23, 1923, issue of *The New York Times Magazine.*—MUSEUM OF THE CITY OF NEW YORK

Ornate metal gateways set in Botticino marble walls led the way to Grand Central's prestigious limited trains. At noon one day in 1933 the gates werè ready for the New Haven's all-parlor car *Knickerbocker Limited* for Boston, and the New York Central's Chicago-bound *Exposition Flyer*, a revival for Chicago's 1933 Century of Progress Exposition of the train of the same name put on for the city's World's Columbian Exposition of 1893.—PENN CENTRAL COMPANY

Grand Central's splendid main waiting room was said to be capable of accommodating 5,000 people. Five huge bronze chandeliers hung from its 50-foot high ceiling. The drawing is from the December 7, 1912, *Scientific American.*—AUTHOR'S COLLECTION

Unlike most stations, the Grand Central design concentrated such functions as ticket windows, baggage and parcel checking, and information in the main concourse, and the terminal's main waiting room off 42nd Street was consequently a much more tranquil space. It was a large room, 65 feet by 205 feet, with a 50-foot high ornate beamed ceiling, finished in materials similar to those used in the main concourse. Five huge bronze chandeliers illuminated the waiting room. Connecting with the main waiting room at opposite ends were separate men's and women's waiting rooms and lavatories. The women's waiting room, at the east end, was finished in quartered oak and included such amenities as a hair dressing salon and shoe shining shop. A barber shop, baths, and private dressing rooms were provided convenient to the men's smoking room.

A separate concourse for the lower level suburban terminal was placed immediately below its upper level counterpart, and was equally large, but without the high ceiling of course. Ticket offices, baggage and parcel rooms, and an information booth were installed at locations corresponding to the upper level arrangement.

A notable feature of the terminal's interior design was the ceiling of thin, shallow terra cotta vaults erected in the space occupied by Grand Central's restaurant and the famous Oyster Bar, on the lower level directly below the main waiting room. Installed by the Spanish artisan Raphael Guastavino, the cream-colored tile vaults gave the rooms an attractive grotto-like effect.

A separate arrival station for long distance trains, linked to the main concourse by an underground passageway, was provided on the terminal's upper level on the west side of Vanderbilt Avenue, beneath the site of the railroad's planned hotel. The separate arrival concourse here was a convenient place to meet friends or relatives, and journalists liked to refer to it as the "kissing gallery."

Incoming and outgoing baggage rooms, adjacent to a cab driveway, were installed at street level in the terminal office building just north of the main concourse. Baggage elevators provided access to two platforms on the upper level designed for the use of solid baggage

A vaulted ceiling of thin Guastavino tile gave Grand Central's lower level restaurant a distinctive air. The famous Oyster Bar opened for business here the same day the terminal did, and remains today one of the better eating places in midtown Manhattan. The drawing is from the December 7, 1912, *Scientific American*.— AUTHOR'S COLLECTION (RIGHT) Charles Reed's wide, gently sloping ramps led large crowds of passengers smoothly between the subway platforms and Grand Central's suburban concourse. It was said, with some exaggeration, that a barrel released through one of the doors on 42nd Street would roll smoothly down the ramp and come to a stop on the concourse in front of a ticket window.—DONALD DUKE COLLECTION

trains, and to a baggage subway one level below the suburban platforms which could be used to transfer baggage to elevators reaching any platform on either level of the terminal.

In commenting on the internal design of Grand Central Robert Anderson Pope, writing in a 1911 issue of *The Town Planning Review* of the University of Liverpool, had noted:

"The essence of the idea that runs through all its designing ... is this: How to build a station so that John Smith or Mary Jones, who have never been in New York, can arrive at the Grand Central Terminal and pass through it to where he or she is going with the least possible confusion and the utmost tranquility and peace of mind. That is really the ideal that has to be sought after in the construction of a great railway terminal nowadays."

In this, Grand Central's architects were notably successful, despite the terminal's great size and the complexity of its multi-level arrangement. Particular attention had been paid to the separation of inbound from outbound traffic, so that passengers and their baggage flowed in an unbroken stream to and from the terminal's dozen different entrances by as direct a route as possible.

The key to the success of Grand Central's internal circulation system was Charles Reed's concept of gently sloping ramps, rather than stairways, to connect the terminal's different levels. Two broad ramps from the corner entrances on 42nd Street, and a third from the subway platforms, led to the suburban concourse. A shallower ramp led from 42nd Street to the main waiting room, which was 3½ feet below street level, and thence to the main concourse, which was about 8 feet below street level. Similar ramps led from

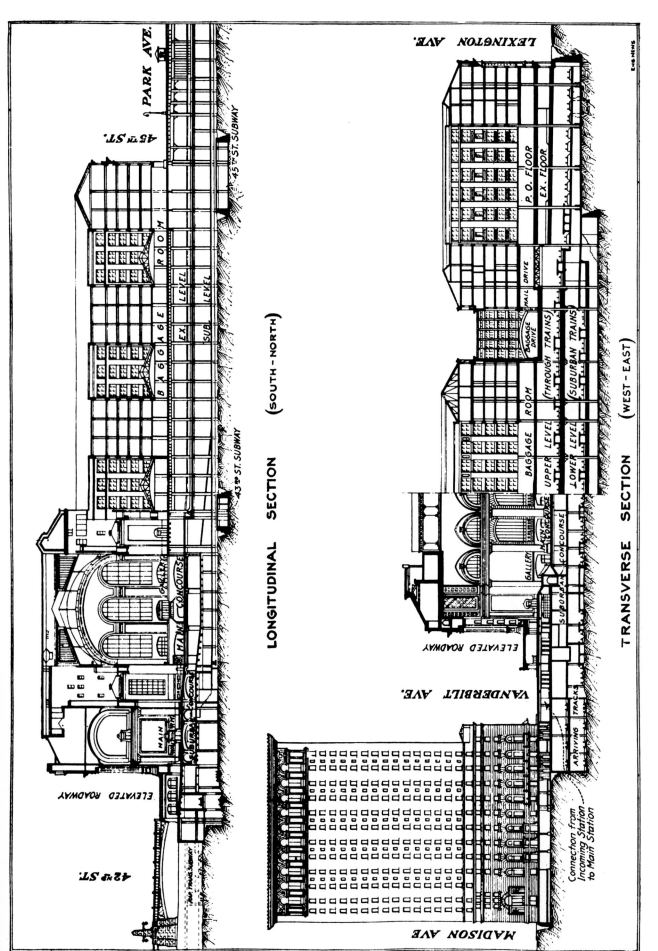

Two sections through the terminal building, reproduced from the May 1, 1913, *Engineering News*, depict the building's complex interior relationships. The south-north longitudinal section shows the relationship of the street level, the two concourses, and the express and suburban level platforms. The westeast transverse section shows the relationship of the main terminal building with the Biltmore Hotel and the arrival station beneath it, and the post office and office building erected between the terminal and Lexington Avenue.—LIBRARY OF CONGRESS

LONGITUDINAL SECTION (SOUTH–NORTH)

TRANSVERSE SECTION (WEST–EAST)

Labels within the longitudinal section: PARK AVE., 45TH ST., 45TH ST. SUBWAY, BAGGAGE ROOM, EX. LEVEL, SUB. LEVEL, 43RD ST. SUBWAY, GALLERY, MAIN CONCOURSE, SUBURBAN CONCOURSE, MAIN, ELEVATED ROADWAY, 42ND ST., TWO-TRACK SUBWAY, Connection from Incoming Station to Main Station, MADISON AVE.

Labels within the transverse section: LEXINGTON AVE., P. O. FLOOR, EX. FLOOR, MAIL DRIVE, BAGGAGE DRIVE, BAGGAGE ROOM, (THROUGH TRAINS), UPPER LEVEL, (SUBURBAN TRAINS), LOWER LEVEL, GALLERY, MAIN CONCOURSE, SUBURBAN CONCOURSE, ELEVATED ROADWAY, VANDERBILT AVE., ARRIVING TRACKS, MADISON AVE.

both the upper and lower level concourses to the platforms, which were at somewhat lower elevations.

Temporary ramps required during the early construction period were installed at different slopes, and the results carefully watched. From this the architects determined that a maximum satisfactory grade was about 10 percent, although those installed in the terminal varied anywhere from about 6 to 11 percent.

Horizontal circulation was provided by an extensive system of underground passageways connecting the different areas of the terminal with each other and with nearby office buildings, hotels, and subway lines.

In keeping with Wilgus' original concepts, the terminal design had made maximum provision for revenue-producing space. The underground passageways were lined with spaces for dozens of shops, the ground floor areas under the elevated roadway that encircled the building provided room for more shops, and still more rentable space was provided within the six-story main terminal building.

Both architectural firms proceeded from their Grand Central collaboration to a variety of other important commissions. Reed & Stem designed the Tacoma (Washington) Union Station of 1909-11, and before the association between the two firms ended following Charles Reed's death, Reed & Stem and Warren & Wetmore collaborated in the design of the Michigan Central station at Detroit, Michigan. The successor firm to Reed & Stem, Fellheimer & Wagner, designed such important stations as the Buffalo (New York) Central Station, the North Station at Boston, Massachusetts and the Cincinnati (Ohio) Union Terminal.

Warren & Wetmore later designed railroad stations at Winnipeg, Manitoba, and Houston, Texas, and a variety of hotels and office buildings at New York and elsewhere. A number of the buildings eventually constructed in the Grand Central District on air rights over the New York Central tracks were designed by Warren & Wetmore.

But by far the best known of the firm's subsequent projects was Whitney Warren's commission for the reconstruction of the great library at the University of Louvain, in Belgium, which had been destroyed by the Germans in 1914. Warren set off a spectacular controversy in this project when he had the inscription *Furore Teutonico Diruta: Dono Americano Restituta* ("Destroyed by German Fury: Restored by American Generosity") placed on the facade of the restored building.*

But whatever their subsequent achievements, for all of the architects engaged in the Grand Central Terminal project, the splendid terminal would remain their greatest work.

---

*An interesting Grand Central footnote to the Louvain inscription controversy is contained in a letter from the writer Elmer Davis to *The New York Times* in 1928, at the height of the uproar. Mr. Davis was obviously not an admirer of Grand Central's 42nd Street facade. "Some of your readers who have been following the controversy over Whitney Warren's inscription on the library at Louvain," he wrote, "could make up their minds about it more easily if they knew whether Mr. Warren, who designed the Grand Central Terminal, is personally responsible for the 'Kolossal' group of statuary over the front door. If that group were *diruta furore Teutonico* ("destroyed by German fury"), or anything else, this would be a brighter and happier town."

Scaffolding still embraced the east facade, and the roof was not yet complete in this May 10, 1912, construction photograph of the main terminal building, taken from a building on the south side of 42nd Street. Less than a year later the building's doors would be thrown open to the public.—PENN CENTRAL COMPANY

5

A Prodigious Task Wonderfully Accomplished

Construction of the new Grand Central Terminal was to prove a task of extraordinary difficulty, requiring as it did the blasting of the great two-level terminal gallery out of Manhattan's granite, the demolition of the old station, and the erection of the new structure in its place, all the while maintaining without interruption a traffic that by this time had grown to more than 1,000 train and switching movements on a busy day. From the time the first work began on the site in July of 1903 until the completed terminal was thrown open to the public early in 1913 the construction was to require just a few months short of a decade.

Between 1903 and 1907 the plans for the terminal yard and its approaches underwent several major revisions and enlargements. The railroad finally purchased additional land, and secured underground rights from the city that permitted the widening of the suburban station under Vanderbilt Avenue and Depew Place. In the end, the site was increased from 23 to almost 48 acres.

As the plan for the terminal evolved in its final form, the upper level for long distance trains would have 32 tracks at platforms. A gradually sloping ramp would carry suburban trains down to the lower level which would have 17 tracks at platforms. Additional tracks were provided on both levels for mail, express, and storage. In all, the terminal tracks could accommodate more than 1,100 cars, over three times the storage capacity of the old Grand Central Station. Loops were planned at the inner end on both levels to permit inbound trains to rapidly turn and clear the terminal after discharging their passengers. On the suburban level provision was made for the later connection of the tracks with the IRT's Park Avenue subway, in accordance with the original Wilgus concept. The terminal yards on both levels extended north to 50th Street, a distance of more than 2,000 feet from 42nd Street, while ten approach tracks fanned out from the four tracks of the Park Avenue tunnel at 57th Street. Six inner approach tracks continued south on a slightly ascending grade of 0.42 percent into the upper level terminal, while the other four, two on each side of Park Avenue, descended on a 2.16

The drama of heavy construction at the Grand Central Terminal site was captured in this drawing by G. W. Peters for the September 1907 issue of *The Century* magazine. Looking south, we see a steam shovel excavating the great gallery for the two-level subterranean terminal along the east side of the construction site. Steam-powered work trains hauled the rock and earth northward for track widening projects on the New York Central's Hudson and Harlem divisions. —AUTHOR'S COLLECTION

percent grade into the suburban terminal.

The excavation of the great gallery or pit for this below ground, two-level terminal and its approaches was one of the most difficult items of construction work. The excavation was anywhere from 23 feet to 46 feet deep, and it was as much as two blocks wide, and a half-mile long. Between 42nd and 50th streets the excavation extended from Lexington Avenue all, or most, of the way to Madison Avenue, and from 50th to 57th streets the terminal approaches occupied an excavation the full width of Park Avenue. Altogether, nearly two million cubic yards of rock, and more than a million cubic yards of earth, had to be dug and blasted from the site.

"It was planned that the yard excavation should be made in three successive 'bites'," wrote Wilgus, "each to be completed before another was undertaken, working westward from Lexington Avenue, so that the traffic of the three railroads using the terminal... might continue without hindrance."

"Bite No. 1," as Wilgus put it, occupied, in part, newly acquired real estate along Lexington Avenue on the east side of the site. The excavation contractor, the O'Rourke Engineering Construction Co., moved onto the site in August 1903 and began the demolition of some 200 buildings along Park and Lexington avenues between 45th and 50th streets. This work complete, and the debris removed, excavation was started with steam shovels. Typically, rock was encountered at around 10 to 20 feet below the surface, which then required drilling and blasting operations. By mid-1912, with nearly 800,000 cubic yards of excavation still remaining, over 750,000 pounds of dynamite had been used in this work.

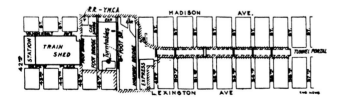

FIG. 2. TERMINAL, 1900-1905

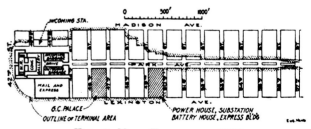

FIG. 3. NEW TERMINAL, 1913

These two sketches from the May 1, 1913, issue of *Engineering News* show how the terminal site was enlarged by the purchase of additional land. At left is shown the original site of some 23 acres; at right is shown the expanded site of almost 48 acres.—LIBRARY OF CONGRESS

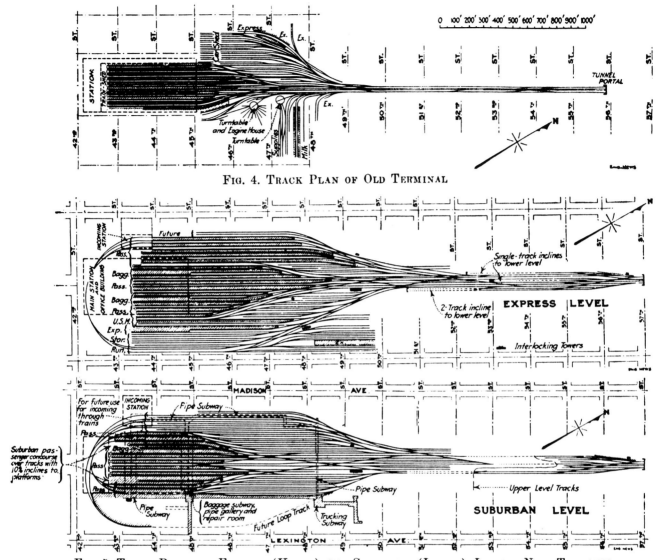

FIG. 4. TRACK PLAN OF OLD TERMINAL

FIG. 5. TRACK PLANS OF EXPRESS (UPPER) AND SUBURBAN (LOWER) LEVELS, NEW TERMINAL

FIGS. 4 AND 5. CONDENSED TRACK PLANS OF GRAND CENTRAL TERMINAL, OLD AND NEW
Another set of sketches from *Engineering News* compares the track plan of the old Grand
Central Station (TOP) with the upper and lower level track plans as they finally evolved in 1913.
The new terminal had 50 tracks at platforms, compared to 19 in the old station, and the
terminal storage capacity was increased by more than three times to a total of more than 1,100
cars.—LIBRARY OF CONGRESS

At the same time, during 1903 and 1904, work proceeded with the widening of the terminal approaches between 50th and 57th streets, and the construction of the new tracks at both levels along the east side of Park Avenue, permitting access to the terminal excavation area by work trains as well as a later connection with the completed express and suburban level tracks in the initial section of the new two-level terminal.

Simultaneously with its suburban electrification project, the New York Central was carrying out an extensive program of yard expansion and an increase in the number of tracks on its Harlem and Hudson division suburban routes. Excavated material from the terminal site was hauled as many as 40 miles to be used as fill material in this work. As many as 55,000 cubic yards of rock were excavated from the site monthly, and more than 400 carloads of rock and earth were hauled out of the site almost every day for years on end.

Even before the excavation could begin, some 25 miles of water lines and sewers had to be removed or relocated, and intercepting

This photograph, reproduced from the September 16, 1905, issue of *Scientific American*, shows excavation work in progress on what chief engineer Wilgus termed "Bite No. 1." Most of the real estate involved in this initial phase of the work was newly acquired, and the old station and its yard had not yet been disturbed. Only some engine storage tracks and milk car platforms, which previously extended through the area where the steam shovel is at work, had given way to the construction forces. (BELOW) Some particularly difficult construction engineering was required in Park Avenue where the railroad's existing four-track tunnel was widened out to the full width of the Avenue to accommodate ten tracks. This photograph from the September 16, 1905, *Scientific American*, facing north from the entrance to the terminal yard, shows the two huge trusses between 56th and 57th streets that supported Park Avenue above the track switches that directed trains into the ten-track approach to the new yard.—BOTH AUTHOR'S COLLECTION

sewers built in Park Avenue from 49th to 54th Street. Drainage from both levels of the subterranean terminal was entirely independent of the city's sewer system, and a special system of pumps and sewers conveyed rainfall and sewage to a new six-foot diameter, brick and concrete outfall sewer dug in 46th Street to the East River, nearly three quarters of a mile away. Much of the sewer was drilled through solid rock, but at Third Avenue quicksand was encountered, necessitating additional construction to support the elevated railway.

Excavation of the Park Avenue cut between 50th and 57th streets necessitated intricate temporary underpinning of the buildings fronting on Park Avenue. An extensive system of "needle beams" had to be installed, for example, to support the walls of the Steinway Piano Factory between 52nd and 53rd streets. Once the excavation was completed, heavy concrete retaining walls, 25 feet high and 12 feet thick at the base, were installed to protect the sides of the cut. The 50,000 cubic yards of concrete required for these walls was placed from a movable concrete mixing plant installed on a railroad car. A tower installed on the car was equipped with an elevator, which delivered concrete materials from attendant supply cars to storage bins which then discharged materials by gravity into the mixing machine.

Between 56th and 57th streets, where the existing four-track tunnel was widened out to the full 140-foot width of Park Avenue to accommodate ten tracks, some intricate structural work was required. In order to permit the placement of track switches without interference from supporting columns, two massive steel trusses were erected at this point to support the tunnel roof. Spanning 150 feet, and 15 feet in depth, the trusses were enclosed in ornamental concrete where they projected above the street level in the landscaped Park Avenue median.

As work proceeded from east to west, each longitudinal "bite" of the new terminal construction was excavated to the required depth and the new two-level terminal tracks then completed. Suburban level tracks were laid on a concrete roadbed resting directly on the rock floor of the excavation, while the upper level tracks were supported by a system of steel

This photograph, facing to the northwest from a point just south of 50th Street, shows the progress of construction at the north end of the new yard during 1907. In the foreground are steel beams for the new multi-level terminal. Just below the temporary bridge that carried 50th Street pedestrian traffic over the excavation can be seen one of the construction locomotives standing in a section of the original yard where excavation has not yet started. The Shaefer Brewery in the right background stood at the corner of 50th Street and Park Avenue.—MUSEM OF THE CITY OF NEW YORK

A splendid glass plate view from the Detroit Publishing Company collection shows the progress of work in 1908 from a vantage point facing south from the 45th Street pedestrian bridge across the terminal yard. In the left foreground is the new post office and railroad office building, constructed above two levels of new terminal tracks already completed and placed in service. Just beyond it is the old Grand Central Palace, which by this time has been converted to a temporary station. In the center foreground a steam shovel is at work on the suburban level.—LIBRARY OF CONGRESS

A second 1908 Detroit Publishing Company view shows the status of work to the north of the 45th Street foot bridge. The completed first section of the two-level terminal is on the right, and structural steel erection is in progress for the viaducts that will carry the cross-town streets across the new yard. To the left a portion of the original ground-level yard is still in use.—LIBRARY OF CONGRESS

In this photograph dated August 5, 1910, we see that yet another section of tracks has been placed in service, and the excavators have advanced westward for one more "bite" of the original yard. By this time all of the tracks in the original station are gone, and only the Vanderbilt Avenue side of the building still stands.—PENN CENTRAL COMPANY

columns and girders, which in turn carried a heavy floor system of steel beams and concrete. The lower portions of steel columns between the tracks were encased in solid concrete piers. Upper column sections and girders were protected by concrete placed on wire lath. Passenger platforms at car floor-level were constructed of reinforced concrete at both express and suburban levels of the terminal. Tracks were supported by creosoted wood blocks set into the concrete roadbed.

As each section of the new two-level terminal was completed, it was placed in service, thereby permitting an adjacent section of the original terminal tracks to be taken out of service and another "bite" of the excavation to be started.

In order to carry on the excavation work the contractor installed a large power plant equipped with a battery of steam boilers and air compressors with a capacity of 5,000 cubic feet of air per minute, which was delivered through a 10-inch main and branches to all parts of the yard area. There were also seven locomotive cranes, four locomotives, 30 steel dump cars, three steam shovels, and a variety of concrete mixers, pumps, and other equipment in use for this work.

To permit the later demolition of the original station, work was started early to establish a temporary station on the Lexington Avenue side of the site. First, a new 13-story loft building was constructed above the new below-ground tracks along Lexington, between 46th and 47th streets. Three floors of this building were given over to a great exhibition hall replacing the old Grand Central Palace at 43rd and Lexington. Then the lower floor of the old Palace was converted to a temporary station. At about the same time, a temporary three-story brick office building was erected on Madison Avenue between 43rd and 44th streets, to accommodate most of the railroad offices in the old station. The remainder were relocated into the old Grand Central Palace. These things done, the demolition of Commodore Vanderbilt's huge train shed and the original Grand Central Station was started in 1908.

Removal of Grand Central's great iron train shed, which covered an area of some 120,000 square feet, was a particularly difficult task. Altogether some 1,700 tons of wrought and cast iron, 150,000 square feet of roofing and

Dating to around 1911, this drawing by Vernon Howe Bailey for *Munsey's Magazine* shows one of the new electric locomotives in a portion of the temporary terminal. Beyond is the new Grand Central Palace between 46th and 47th streets.— LIBRARY OF CONGRESS

glass, and more than half a million bricks had to be taken down, all of it while normal traffic continued on the terminal tracks below. An enormous moving platform, or traveler, built to conform to the curve of the train shed's great arches, was used for the work. Sections of the shed were demolished during the day, and the debris laid on the platforms of the traveler. At night, the material was lowered into freight cars for removal. Temporary canopies of wood were then erected over the terminal tracks to provide shelter until the time came to remove these tracks for excavation of the new below-ground terminal.

Throughout the construction period, the railroad was obliged to keep open the foot bridges that carried pedestrians across the old terminal yards along the alignment of the interrupted crosstown streets, a requirement that necessitated some ingenious engineering. At 45th Street, for instance, an excavation 70 feet deep was required for the installation of a baggage subway beneath both levels of the future terminal. In order to clear the excavation area of the many supporting columns for the 45th Street pedestrian foot bridge and a 36-inch diameter gas main that crossed at this location, the railroad's engineers suspended the foot bridge and gas main from a 172-foot-long wooden truss. Mounted on wheels, the truss was advanced from east to west as the excavation progressed. Permanent steel viaducts for the restored crosstown streets were erected simultaneously with the construction of each section of the two-level terminal.

Demolition of the old station in 1910 was followed immediately by excavation of the site and the erection of the new terminal building. The new building was of steel frame construction, faced with granite and limestone, and required, in all, some 29,000 tons of structural steel. Generally, the building was designed for a conventional arrangement of steel columns and girders, with closely spaced secondary floor beams and short-span concrete floor arches. This was greatly complicated, however, by the restrictions on column placement that were imposed by the upper and lower level track plans.

At many locations an irregular spacing of columns was necessitated by the track layouts. Far more difficult were the problems caused

These photographs, both taken in September 1911, record the progress of construction on the main terminal building. The photograph on the left faces north across what will eventually become the main concourse toward the Grand Central Terminal Building, already nearing completion. The view at the right shows structural steel erection for the main terminal's east facade, which will eventually be enclosed in Stony Creek granite and Bedford Limestone.—BOTH MUSEUM OF THE CITY OF NEW YORK

by the dissimilarity between the upper and lower level track plans, which at many locations precluded the erection of columns continuous through both levels. In these cases columns on the upper levels were supported by heavy steel girders spanning between columns on the lower level. At some locations, where columns were designed to support the future erection of a 23-story office building above the terminal, these girders were of exceptionally heavy construction. The heaviest girders in the building, built up of steel plates and angles, were 10 feet deep and weighed nearly 1,800 pounds per linear foot. Among the largest steel columns were several designed to carry loads of more than 2,400 tons, which had a cross sectional area of 371 square inches, and themselves weighed up to 44 tons.

In some of the earliest sections of the structure erected, no attempt was made to keep the columns for the building independent of those for the track-floor framing. Subsequently, when the office portion of the building was completed and trains were being operated on the girder-supported express level, it was found that noticeable vibration was transmitted to the building. This problem was largely resolved by installing longitudinal walls between the columns at both track

levels, and in all further steel design building columns were kept independent of those supporting the track-floor framing wherever possible. At some locations this was done by erecting columns in groups of threes, with the outer two carrying the girders for the track floor, while the middle column passed through the floor, with a slight clearance around it, to support the frame of the building above. At other locations designed for the erection of buildings above the tracks at a later date, the building columns were located midway between the track-floor columns, and were placed through holes cut in the concrete floor.

In order to control Grand Central's complex, two-level track layout, which comprised a total of some 33 miles of track, the railroad installed what was then one of the largest and most advanced signal and interlocking systems ever built. The installation actually consisted of what were essentially five separate all-electric interlocking plants. The two largest, towers A and B, were installed in two-story structures on the terminal's upper and lower levels near 49th Street. Tower A contained a 362-lever interlocking plant controlling most of the express level switches and signals south of 54th Street. Tower B, immediately below Tower A, had a 400-lever plant which similarly controlled most of the switches and signals on the suburban level. Control wires from towers A and B led to ten remote sub-interlocking machines, six on the upper and four on the lower level, from which the switch machines were in turn controlled.

Tower C controlled switches for the upper level yard south of 50th Street and just west of Lexington Avenue, while Tower F on the lower level controlled switches and signals for the loop tracks on both levels. Tower U at 57th Street housed a 144-lever interlocking machine which controlled the approaches to the terminal.

Three-position dwarf semaphore signals were used throughout the terminal area.

Rearrangement of the approaches to Grand Central and the installation of new signal and interlocking systems finally made it possible for the New York Central to discontinue the left-hand running that had prevailed south of Spuyten Duyvil and White Plains (and, later, Croton Falls) since 1888. Work on the revised approaches and the new signal and interlocking systems was sufficiently advanced to permit the change to orthodox right-hand operation in 1907.

Between 49th and 50th streets on Lexington Avenue the railroad erected a building which housed a large substation and storage battery installation for the electrification, and another for boilers and generating equipment that supplied heat and lighting current to the entire terminal area. An extensive forced air ventilation system was built to supply the two terminal levels, the main station, and its adjacent office building. Piping systems supplied water, compressed air, steam, and vacuum throughout the terminal yard. A fire protection piping system with some 300 hose connections extended throughout the terminal, and an alarm system with 125 call boxes was connected both to the terminal's own fire department and the city's fire department.

The long and difficult construction period was marked by frequent change and controversy. As has already been noted, the design for both the terminal trackage and the terminal building itself underwent several major redesigns during the course of the work. Indeed, substantial revisions to the plans were still being made as late as 1911.

Early in 1907, only three days after the opening of the railroad's new suburban electrification, which had been carried out under Wilgus' supervision, one of the new electric trains derailed and overturned in The Bronx, with heavy loss of life. In subsequent testimony before the New York Railroad Commission, Wilgus became engaged in a public controversy with the railroad's vice president and general manager, A. H. Smith, over the responsibility for the accident. Although no conclusive determination was ever reached, Wilgus resigned his position soon afterward, leaving to others the task of completing his great work.

Whatever the reasons for his departure from the New York Central, Wilgus went on to continue his distinguished career as a consulting engineer. As chairman of the advisory board of engineers for the Michigan Central Railroad's Detroit River Tunnel, completed in 1910, Wilgus devised an innovative system of construction under which prefabricated tunnel sections were lowered into place in a trench in the river floor. For this achievement he was awarded the Telford Gold Medal of the Institute of Civil Engineers of Great Britain. As a U.S. Army colonel, he was director of military railways in the American Expeditionary Force during World War I. Shortly after the war, as chairman of a board of engineers studying a New York-New Jersey crossing of the Hudson River, he had an early role in the planning of the Holland Tunnel. Rich with honors, he died at Claremont, New Hampshire, on October 24, 1949, at the age of 83 years.

Succeeding Wilgus in overall charge of the Grand Central project was George A. Harwood, chief engineer of electric zone improvements, who continued in that position until the completion of construction.

The construction work itself was remarkably free of serious accidents, although the site was the scene of a spectacular and disastrous explosion in December 1910 that was not directly related to the construction effort. A train being switched into a yard track near 50th Street, in order to have its supply of Pintsch gas for car lighting replenished, over-ran a bumping post and ruptured a gas line. Gas leaked into the nearby power substation for the railroad's electrification, resulting in an explosion so fierce that the building was almost completely demolished, a nearby streetcar was overturned, and an estimated $25,000 worth of plate glass windows were blown out in the vicinity. Ten people were killed and over 100 seriously injured. The accident hastened the replacement of Pintsch lighting with electric light systems on the New York Central.

By 1911 work on the new terminal building and its related office structure was sufficiently advanced to permit offices in the temporary building on Madison Avenue to be relocated to the new building, and the Madison Avenue building torn down. By October 1912 the new building had progressed far enough to permit opening of the suburban level terminal, and within a few more months the great terminal was, to all practical purposes, fully completed, although several important features were not finished until much later. The separate arrival station was not opened until 1914, the terminal loop tracks were not complete on both levels until 1927, and the elevated roadway that carried Park Avenue traffic around the terminal building was not finished in its entirety until 1929.

By the beginning of February 1913, all was in readiness for the opening of the splendid new terminal. During the afternoon and evening of Saturday, February 1, some 2,000 guests of the architects inspected the terminal, and a guest list of a hundred was entertained by Whitney Warren and Charles Wetmore at a dinner in the station restaurant. The principal rooms of the station were decorated with palms, and a band was on hand. Precisely at midnight the doors were thrown open to the public and a crowd of about 3,000 persons, which had been waiting outside, rushed in. All day Sunday, February 2, the building was jammed with sightseers. By 7 P.M. that evening more than 150,000 people had inspected the newest and grandest of all railroad terminals.

The new terminal received extraordinarily wide coverage and extravagant praise in the press. Both the New York *Evening Post* and *The New York Times,* for example, published special opening day supplements devoted to detailed description of the new terminal and

Civil engineer George A. Harwood, the New York Central's chief engineer of electric zone improvements, took charge of the Grand Central Terminal construction following William J. Wilgus' resignation in 1907. He continued in that position until the project's completion, and later became the railroad's vice president in charge of improvements and development. When the great terminal was completed and opened to the public on February 2, 1913, Harwood received the receipt shown below for the building signed by A. R. Whaley, the railroad's general superintendent electric division; Miles Bronson, superintendent electric division; and terminal manager W. L. Morse, revealing a sense of humor not usually associated with high offials of a great railroad company. — BOTH HERBERT H. HARWOOD COLLECTION

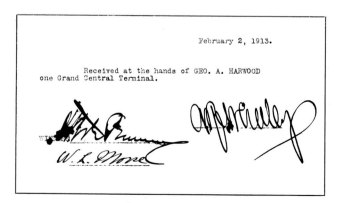

The New York Central was inordinately proud of its splendid new terminal, and Grand Central's completion was widely advertised in journals of national circulation. This full page "The Terminal City" ad in the January 25, 1913, *Harper's Weekly* proclaimed it "the greatest civic development ever undertaken."

its construction. *The Times* described the project as solving the "greatest terminal problem of the age." *Scientific American* called the terminal "a monumental gateway to America's greatest city."

But perhaps, considering the enormous difficulties that its construction presented, the completed Grand Central was best described in the words of William Inglis in an article for the February 1st issue of *Harper's Weekly* as, "... the consumation of a prodigious task wonderfully accomplished."

Certainly in its operational features the new terminal, together with the railroad's new suburban electrification, constituted a remarkable improvement over those of the old. The

electrification, of course, solved the hazardous operating problems that had been created in the Park Avenue tunnel by the smoke and gases of steam locomotives, and simultaneously eliminated a source of the most intense public disaffection with the railroad. The great improvement in operating flexibility afforded by both the availability of the terminal loops and the use of multiple unit electric suburban trains, as well as the greatly increased storage capacity provided by the enlarged, two-level terminal, substantially reduced the requirement for terminal switching and the volume of "deadhead" empty equipment moves between Grand Central and the Mott Haven yard north of the Harlem River. The latter improvement was particularly important, for the four-track Park Avenue approach to the Grand Central now constituted the most severe constraint on the ultimate traffic capacity of the terminal.

The tremendous increase in capacity afforded by the New York Central's terminal improvements became available none too soon. In 1900 the old station had handled an annual traffic of 106,000 trains and some 13,600,000 passengers. By 1910 this traffic had increased to 130,000 trains and more than 20 million passengers annually, and by 1920 Grand Central's annual passenger traffic would reach a level of more than 37 million.

In the end, the costs for the project far outstripped the original estimates of 1903. The final cost for the work, including the terminal, its yard, the suburban electrification and track improvements, and some revenue-producing facilities, was somewhere around $72 million. Even this figure excluded the costs of the additional land purchases required for the project, and included among the revenue-producing facilities only those included in the terminal building itself and the railroad-owned Biltmore Hotel.

But in the light of its great benefits to the New York Central, and its enormously beneficial effects on the subsequent growth of New York City and its suburban neighbors to the north, there can be no doubt that the railroad's great expenditure for this masterful work of engineering and architecture was to prove an exceptionally timely and productive investment.

6

A City Within a City

Considered on almost any level the Grand Central Terminal was to prove an extraordinarily successful project. As a work of engineering it was an inspired solution to an exceptionally difficult set of site conditions and operating requirements. And the architectural design of the terminal structure was both an innovative solution to the functional problems of a very large terminal and an aesthetically pleasing work that continues to receive high praise more than a half century after its completion.

But it is as a brilliant and pioneering work of urban development that Grand Central achieved its greatest success. For Wilgus' concept of air rights development above the terminal tracks and commercial development within the terminal itself; the great effectiveness with which the design integrated railroad, subway, and surface transportation; and its efficient system of horizontal and vertical circulation of pedestrian traffic all combined to make Grand Central the center and catalyst

of a dynamic development and growth of a major urban area of mid-town Manhattan. It is in this capacity that Grand Central Terminal most clearly stands apart from all other similar projects.

Grand Central's urban significance was recognized from the beginning. It was, declared *The New York Times* in its February 2, 1913, opening day issue, "... more than a gateway, more than a terminal. The terminal proper, the great head house and its accompanying buildings, are simply the heart and the cause of a group of buildings that has best been described as a 'terminal city'."

Within the terminal itself there was an extraordinary variety of enterprises. Dozens of shops located within the building's commercial space offered almost any service or merchandise one could want; today there are some some 140 of them. There were restaurants, a post office, a movie theater, and an emergency hospital, complete with a physician in attendance. The railroad had its own terminal

Grand Central Terminal formed a nucleus for the dynamic growth and development of the mid-town Manhattan area around it. Some of the vitality of 42nd Street and Park Avenue is suggested by this 1934 Vernon Howe Bailey drawing from his *Magical City*. Motor traffic is heavy on the elevated approach that led to the circumferential roadway around the terminal which linked upper and lower Park Avenue. The streetcar below is about to enter the tunnel under Park Avenue that once carried New York & Harlem trains. Across the street is the Pershing Square Building which rose on the site of the old Grand Union Hotel a few years after the new Grand Central was completed. Beyond the terminal, from right to left, are glimpses of the Graybar Building, the tip of one of the Waldorf-Astoria Hotel towers, and the New York Central Building, all of which were erected on air rights over the terminal tracks. (BELOW) A drawing from the January-February 1968 issue of *The Architectural Forum* shows how Grand Central's extraordinary circulation system had evolved by the late 1960's. The terminal's undergound walkway system, shown in light black, served 21 different buildings, shown in white. Rail and subway lines are in dark black.—AUTHOR'S COLLECTION

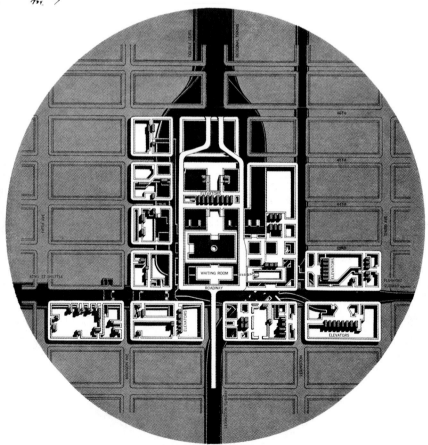

police department. Within the six-story main terminal building there was still more rentable space. Among its tenants over the years have been such diverse establishments as an art gallery, clubs, a gymnasium and tennis courts, a photo studio, Columbia Broadcasting System studios, and meeting rooms. For many years Grand Central even had an artist—Vincent Maragliotti—at work in its giant attic, where he painted, appropriately enough, outsize murals. Private dressing rooms were available so that suburbanites could change from street clothes to evening dress, and for many years a wealthy suburban couple, Mr. and Mrs. John W. Campbell, maintained a luxurious apartment off the terminal's west balcony so that they could take a train into town and entertain city friends conveniently. By day the elegantly furnished room doubled as Campbell's office. In more recent years the apartment has become a rather splendid office for the terminal's police superintendent.

People were fond of saying that you could spend days without ever going outside Grand Central and still satisfy almost any want. And there was even an old tale about a fugitive who once evaded police for two years without ever leaving Grand Central. It probably wasn't true, but it could have been.

The different areas of the terminal and its commercial development were connected with each other and with nearby office buildings, hotels, and subways by Grand Central's complex system of ramps and underground passageways. Without ever emerging aboveground a pedestrian could reach buildings as far south as 41st Street and as far north as 46th, and along three blocks of 42nd Street from Third Avenue to Madison; today there are some 21 buildings that can be reached through this splendid circulation system.

Provision was made for direct access from the new Grand Central to four levels of subway tracks. Already in place was the four-track line of the IRT, which ran under 42nd Street from Broadway to Grand Central, where it turned south under Park Avenue. At the lowest level was the Manhattan terminal of the New York & Long Island Railroad, popularly known as the Steinway Tunnels, a trolley subway line that extended under the

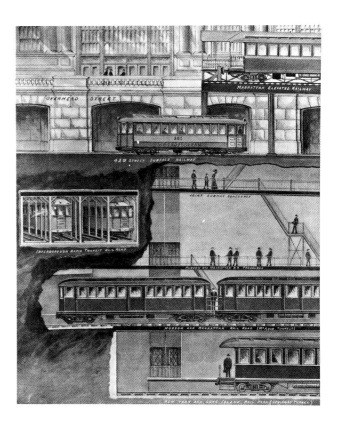

This cutaway drawing from the November 19, 1910, issue of *Scientific American* shows the multiple levels of New York's rail transit system that were planned for Grand Central's front door. The H&M line was never built, and the Steinway Tunnel on the lower level became part of the IRT subway system. Another cutaway (BELOW) from the December 7, 1912, *Scientific American Supplement* shows how the joint subway concourse was linked directly with the terminal's system of internal ramps and passageways, and the relationship of the subways to the terminal's express and suburban train loops.—BOTH AUTHOR'S COLLECTION

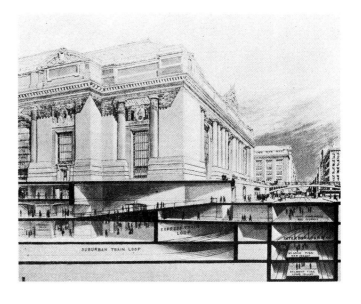

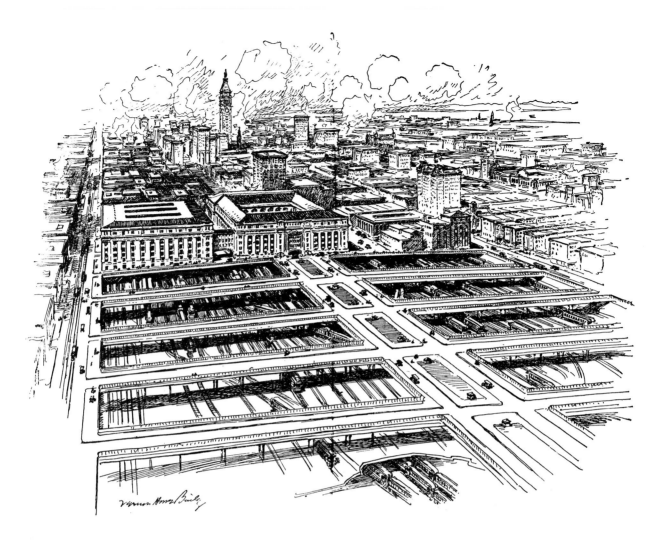

Two drawings by artist Vernon Howe Bailey for the January 12, 1907, *Harper's Weekly* illustrate the expected air rights development above Grand Central's subterranean yard. This aerial view looking south from about 50th Street shows the extent of the area above the yard that was to be made available for development. Buildings were omitted in order to show how the restored crosstown streets would span the tracks. Another view looking south toward the new terminal (LEFT) shows how the transformed Park Avenue was expected to be flanked by harmonious buildings. Park Avenue did indeed grow into a splendid thoroughfare, but not like this.—BOTH DONALD DUKE COLLECTION

This view, facing north from 43rd and Lexington shows the planned construction of post office, express, and railroad office building spaces above the tracks along the eastern front of the terminal development. Only a portion of the building shown here was erected, between 44th and 45th streets, and the Graybar Building later occupied the site in the foreground.—DONALD DUKE COLLECTION

East River to Queens. Although completed in 1907, the latter was not opened for regular service until 1915 because of legal disputes with the city; when it finally opened it was as part of the IRT subway system. At intermediate levels plans were made for later connections to the planned Lexington Avenue subway, which opened in 1918, and to a projected extension of the Hudson & Manhattan Railway's uptown line north to Grand Central from its terminal at 33rd Street and Broadway. The H&M extension, however, was never completed.

Still other connections to Manhattan's urban transportation system were provided by street railway lines in 42nd Street and lower Park Avenue, and a branch from the Third Avenue line of the Manhattan Elevated Railway, which terminated in 42nd Street directly in front of Grand Central.

By depressing the terminal tracks below street level, and re-establishing the crosstown streets on bridges above the tracks, an area of 30 city blocks of some of the world's most valuable real estate had been made available for "air rights" development. Even in 1913 it was estimated that the real estate alone in each city block in this part of Manhattan was worth two to three million dollars; today it is worth perhaps twenty million dollars.

Development of this newly-available real estate began even before construction of the terminal was completed, and the New York Central set up a subsidiary company to take care of rentals and its other real estate business. By the time the new Grand Central opened early in 1913, structures had been put up, or at least planned, on almost half of the available air rights above the terminal tracks.

The Grand Central Palace, which was to rank for many years as one of New York's largest exhibition halls, occupied most of the block bounded by 46th and 47th streets, and Lexington and Park avenues. The railroad's heating and power plant facilities and the Adams Express Company occupied most of a similarly-sized block between 49th and 50th streets. On Lexington Avenue, between 44th and 45th streets, the railroad erected a six-story building that housed a post office on the lower floors, with office spaces on the upper floors. The New York Central's general

Completion of Grand Central set in motion a construction boom in the surrounding area that continued without interruption for two decades. This Vernon Howe Bailey drawing from the November 1916 *Scribner's Magazine* shows the construction then underway on the southeast corner of 42nd and Park Avenue, where the Pershing Square Building was taking the place of the venerable Grand Union Hotel. Visible in the left background is a corner of the Belmont Hotel, while in the background beyond the terminal are the Vanderbilt Avenue Office Building and the Biltmore Hotel, both built above the terminal tracks. (BELOW) One of the Grand Central District's first major air rights developments was the railroad-owned Bilmore Hotel, which was erected above Grand Central's arrival station on Vanderbilt Avenue. Opened in 1914, the Biltmore quickly established itself as one of New York's leading hotels, a distinction that it retains to this day.—BOTH DONALD DUKE COLLECTION

office building was erected a few years later in the adjacent block, between 45th and 46th streets. The Grand Central Terminal Building, housing additional office spaces, was constructed just to the north of the main terminal building, fronting on 45th Street.

Already under construction at the time of the terminal's opening was the Biltmore Hotel, which occupied the block just to the west of the main terminal building from Vanderbilt Avenue to Madison Avenue, and extending between 43rd and 44th streets. Located directly above the terminal's arrival tracks, the hotel incorporated Grand Central's separate arrival station into its basement and first floor; it was possible for an arriving passenger to take an elevator directly from the arrival concourse to the hotel lobby. Journalists of the time made much of the fact that a Chicago businessman, by staying at the Biltmore and taking advantage of Grand Central's direct connections to the subways, could travel all the way from Chicago, put up at a hotel, and conduct his business on Wall Street "without ever having put his head out of doors in New York."

Owned by the railroad, the Biltmore was intended to be one of New York's most prestigious deluxe hotels, and the company secured Gustav Baumann, long identified with the elegant Holland House on Fifth Avenue, to preside over the new hotel's destinies. Among the Biltmore's notable features was its 23rd floor grand ballroom and dining room, which could be opened into an open-air roof garden on warm summer evenings. "From a table there," reported *The New York Times*, "milord and his lady can look out to the dark stretch of Central Park to the north, and to the south the Metropolitan tower and far away the tip of the Woolworth Building; to the west the Times Building, and beyond the Hudson and the Jersey shore, and to the east the East River and Long Island."

Just to the north of the Biltmore, the new Yale Club building was under construction, and other planned projects included buildings for the Racquet and Tennis Club and the Railroad Y.M.C.A. A second major railroad-owned hotel, the 2,000-room Commodore, was planned for the corner of 42nd Street and Lexington Avenue. Delayed while the alignment of the Lexington Avenue subway through the building site was worked out, the Commodore was completed in 1919.

One of the most beneficial results of the construction of the terminal and the conversion of the New York Central's train operations from steam to electric motive power was the spectacular transformation of upper Park Avenue from a sooty, dingy right-of-way for the railroad's intense Manhattan traffic into one of the city's most prestigious thoroughfares. As writer Arthur Bartlett

For a few years, before air rights development above the terminal yard was complete, trains still left in daylight from Grand Central's express level platforms. The New York Central's premier, all-Pullman *Twentieth Century Limited* waited for its early afternoon departure time on June 10, 1914.—Penn Central Company (below) A New York Central T motor heads an outbound train past a lineup of idle New Haven electric motors. —Eric H. Archer Collection

Opened in 1929, the New York Central Building between 45th and 46th streets completed the north end of the grouping of buildings along the centerline of Park Avenue between 42nd and 46th streets. In this northward-facing view from south of 42nd Street, the ornate 35-story building looms above the low terminal building. Visible beyond it to the right is the twin-towered Waldorf-Astoria Hotel at Park Avenue and 50th Street.—DAVID V. HYDE, FROM PENN CENTRAL COMPANY

Maurice noted in his commentary to Vernon Howe Bailey's *Magical City,* "The story of Park Avenue is the old story of Cinderella—yesterday a kitchen drudge of a street, today a resplendent Princess; and the Fairy Godmother who waved the wand and wrought the change was electrification."

From 45th Street north, Park Avenue had been restored as a splendid boulevard some 140 feet wide, and the planners of what the railroad's publicists like to call "a new civic center" envisioned the harmonious development of grand new hotels, apartment houses, commercial structures, and public buildings along the elegant avenue. This great design was to be largely realized, although a few of the grander projects never materialized, among them an ambitious vision of upper Park Avenue opening into a great plaza—rivaling Paris' Place de l'Opera—with a splendid new house for the Metropolitan Opera at its center.

Air rights development along the newly-created section of Park Avenue above 45th Street was completed by the end of the 1920's. There were a number of major office buildings and luxury apartment buildings. The Marguery and Park Lane hotels were constructed on Park Avenue, while the Roosevelt, Barclay, and Chatham hotels were built just off the avenue.

By far the most important new tenant in the newly-fashionable upper Park Avenue district, however, was the celebrated Waldorf-Astoria Hotel, which in 1929 began construction of its new building on the block bounded by 49th and 50th streets, and Lexington and Park avenues, originally occupied by the railroad's terminal power plant. Its location above the tracks permitted the celebrated hostelry the unique distinction of its own railroad side track in the basement, so to speak. Officially identified as Track 61 in one of Grand Central's storage yards, with a freight elevator providing access to the hotel, the siding was used on occasion for the arrival or departure of distinguished guests traveling by private railroad cars.

General John J. Pershing was the first to use it, on a visit to the city in 1938. During the 1944 campaign Franklin D. Roosevelt gave a foreign policy address at the Waldorf and then descended into the "basement" to the presidential rail car for the journey home to Hyde Park. On other occasions the siding has been used for such diverse affairs as a 1946 "debut at the Waldorf" for a new 6,000 horsepower diesel locomotive, or for a 1965 "underground party" for pop artist Andy Warhol.

The real capstone to the transformation of upper Park Avenue came in 1929 with the completion of the 34-story New York Central Building, which stood squarely astride the Park Avenue centerline between 45th and 46th streets. With its construction the railroad was finally able to achieve the upper Park Avenue "Court of Honor" concept originally conceived by architect Charles Reed in 1903, although on a much-modified and less

This drawing by Vernon Howe Bailey from this *Magical City* illustrates how the New York Central electrification transformed upper Park Avenue. The handsome Racquet and Tennis Club building at 370 Park, designed in the Italian Renaissance style by McKim, Mead & White, went up in 1918 where there had been only a smoky railroad yard a few years before.

Set squarely astride Park Avenue between 45th and 46th streets, the New York Central Building was pierced by twin archways which permitted auto traffic to pass to and from Grand Central's circumferential driveway from upper Park Avenue. The statuary group and clock on the building's north facade, although less grandiose, suggested those on the terminal's south facade.

An aerial photograph of the Grand Central District, dating to about 1939, shows the extraordinary transformation wrought in the area above the terminal tracks by a quarter century of air rights development. The buildings in white are those built on air rights. Compare this view with that shown in the drawing on page 96.—

ambitious scale. When the terminal was opened in 1913, Reed's "circumferential plaza" that was to carry elevated traffic lanes for Park Avenue around the building had only been completed on the south and west sides of the terminal, and ended with a grade connection with Park Avenue at 45th Street. The viaduct across 42nd Street was not completed until 1919. With the construction of the New York Central Building the traffic lanes were completed around the east side of the terminal as well, and the elevated roadway extended across 45th Street and through two great arched openings in the new building to descend finally to the Park Avenue grade at 46th.

In the immediate vicinity of the terminal, new office buildings had filled the remaining parcels of railroad-owned property on the west

Two more drawings from Bailey's *Magical City* depict some of the development that appeared in mid-town Manhattan after Grand Central opened. (ABOVE) Prestigious apartment houses rose along upper Park Avenue as soon as steam locomotives were banished. (BELOW) Looming above older buildings in this view from lower Park Avenue are, left to right, the towers of new office buildings of the New York Trust Company at 40th and Madison Avenue, No. 295 Madison at 41st Street, and the Lincoln Building on 42nd Street.

side of Vanderbilt Avenue. On Lexington Avenue the Graybar Building had been built on the block just north of the Commodore in 1926.

The influence of the Grand Central development extended far beyond the immediate confines of the terminal construction area. By 1930 new luxury apartments and town houses extended north along Park Avenue as far as 96th Street, and land values on the Avenue had increased by over 200 percent from the 1914 level. New development extended along the east-west axis of 42nd Street as well. By 1920 many of New York's fashionable stores had relocated into the area between Grand Central and Fifth Avenue. To the east of the terminal along 42nd Street, important earlier developments in the Grand Central District included the Bowery Savings Bank building, opened in 1923; the Chrysler and New York Daily News buildings, completed in 1930 and 1931; and the Tudor City apartment and hotel complex overlooking the East River, which was constructed during 1927-1932.

The magnitude of the development is perhaps best conveyed by the change in the assessed value of real estate in the area around Grand Central over this period. From 1904 to 1930 the value of property in the area between 42nd and 96th streets, and bounded by Lexington and Madison avenues, increased by a billion dollars to a total of $1,268 million. This constituted an increase of 374 percent over the 26-year period, more than double that for Manhattan as a whole.

The ability to incorporate future growth and change was a fundamental feature of the Wilgus plan for the Grand Central complex, yet even Wilgus himself could probably have visualized but dimly the demands that would successfully be placed on it for more than a half century after its completion.

New subway lines, growth in commuter traffic, the construction of additional buildings in the terminal complex itself, and the intense commercial building density that developed in the entire uptown district centering around Grand Central all brought additional pedestrian traffic into the area. By the late 1930's it was estimated that half a million people passed through Grand Central daily.

As far back as 1929, when the New York

A view to the north from Park Avenue and 40th Street shows how both Grand Central and the tower of the New York Central Building stood squarely astride the Park Avenue centerline.

A modern version of the popular Grand Central cutaway drawing, from the January-February 1968 issue of *The Architectural Forum*, shows the additional circulation features installed at the time of the Pan Am Building construction. A bank of escalators linked Grand Central's main concourse to the main lobby of the Pan Am Building, which doubled as a pedestrian concourse extending all the way to 45th Street.—AUTHOR'S COLLECTION

Central Building was erected just north of the terminal on 46th Street, it was said to occupy Grand Central's last available building site. Yet a steady growth of urban activity in the Grand Central district has continued unabated, as new—and much larger—office towers have replaced many of the apartment and office buildings originally built above Grand Central's tracks. In 1963, for example, the 59-story Pan Am Building—then the world's largest commercial office building—was erected just north of Grand Central's main concourse, taking the place of the

six-story terminal office building. Linked directly to the Grand Central concourse by a bank of escalators, the Pan Am Building added 2.4 million square feet and 17,500 new office workers to the Grand Central complex, and drew an estimated 250,000 people daily into the terminal's circulation system.

Yet somehow the vast and brilliant system of horizontal and vertical movement centering around Grand Central's main concourse was able to readily absorb all of this additional pedestrian traffic. And as recently as 1968, when it was more than a half century old, urban designer Frank Williams was able to note in an *Architectural Forum* article that Grand Central's remarkable circulation system "... remains today the most advanced urban 'mixing chamber' in existence."

That this is so is the key to the continued vitality of the Grand Central District, and an extraordinary tribute to the far-sighted and innovative work of its designers.

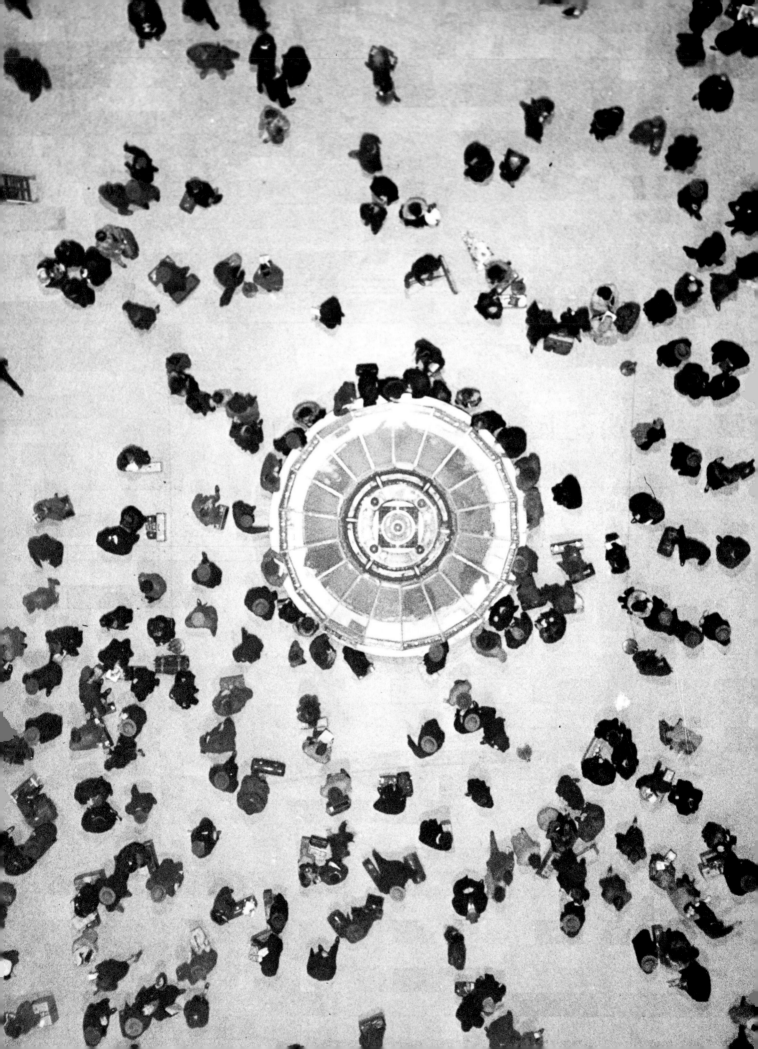

7

Gateway to a Continent

For close to four decades after Grand Central's completion, the great limiteds were to remain the premiére means of American overland public transportation. Every day the New York Central and the New Haven dispatched such distinguished name trains as the *Empire State Express,* the *Wolverine,* the *Southwestern Limited,* the *Yankee Clipper,* or the *Montreal Limited* from Grand Central's subterranean platforms for their diverse destinations in New England, Canada, or the American Middle West. And every afternoon the Central's famous maroon carpet was rolled out for the departure, usually in multiple sections, of that doyenne of American limiteds, the *20th Century Limited.*

In those golden years of the American passenger train the passenger lists of the great limiteds that arrived and departed from Grand Central's express level platforms constituted a "Who's Who" of the socially prominent, the wealthy, and the powerful in American life. The Central's trains enjoyed the favor of the celebrities of sports, the theater, the

concert hall, and the then-new movies, and for decades on end the ritual publicity photograph taken in the gloom of Grand Central on the observation platform of the *Century* or one of its contemporaries on the New York Central timecard was a recognized cachet of celebrity-hood.

If they lacked the glamour of the limiteds on the upper level, the arrivals and departures of the utilitarian suburban trains on Grand Central's lower lever were no less important to the fortunes of the New York Central and the New Haven. The massive enhancement to the capacity, the speed, and the attractiveness of the suburban services of the two railroads that was afforded by the new terminal facilities and electrification helped to bring about an extraordinary growth of the suburban territory north of New York. Between 1906 and 1930 the combined suburban traffic of the two roads grew from an annual total of less than 10 million to nearly 36 million passengers. In Westchester County, just north of New York City, assessed property values grew by more

Grand Central was truly, as the New York Central chose to call it, the "gateway to a continent," and the terminal's great main concourse was its crossroads and meeting place. This classic scene of activity on the concourse dates to 1938.—DAVID V. HYDE, FROM PENN CENTRAL COMPANY.

The New York Central daily rolled out a red carpet for the arrival and departure of the *20th Century Limited*, a mark of distinction for *Century* passengers that was duplicated nowhere else in American railroading. Originally the railroad used a plain Harvard red carpet, later replaced by a buff runner with maroon borders. In this 1941 photograph, on the opposite page, two Grand Central porters roll out a third variation of the design which featured the train's name woven into a maroon background. This pattern came in with the streamlined *Century* of 1938.—DAVID V. HYDE, FROM PENN CENTRAL COMPANY

In a time when the great long distance trains still reigned supreme in American overland transportation, the departure of the New York Central's train-of-trains, the *20th Century Limited*, brought a daily rush of excitement to Grand Central's express platforms. In this 1920's view at the train gate for the *Century's* first section the stylishly attired "passengers" are evidently models posed for some now-forgotten publicity or advertising purpose, but in any event sartorial distinction was the norm for the *Century's* clientelle.—PENN CENTRAL COMPANY

than a billion and a half dollars—an increase of over 800 percent—over the period from 1904 to 1930. There were many reasons for this, of course, but the availability of high quality suburban services was undoubtedly a principal catalyst for this remarkable growth.

At the time of its completion, Grand Central was accommodating a combined total of more than 23 million suburban and long-haul passengers annually. Its builders said it was good for 100 million a year, although it never quite came to that. By 1929, the high water mark of the great heavyweight steel limiteds, the terminal had doubled its passenger load to nearly 47 million a year.

But it was the second World War and the great floodtide of railroad passenger travel that followed it, before the airplane ended it all for good, that brought the greatest crowds of all to Grand Central. The terminal's biggest year ever came as recently as 1946, when over 63 million passengers passed through its gates. Some 550 regular trains entered or left the terminal daily then, and during the peak hour of the evening rush, between 5 and 6 P.M., trains arrived or departed on an average of a minute apart.

Grand Central was far from being the world's greatest terminal from the point of view of traffic. In 1913, for instance, the year Grand Central opened, Boston's South Station—then the busiest in the United States—handled almost three quarters again as many passengers as Grand Central, and more than twice as many trains. But there was never any real question about the fact that Grand Central was the best known railroad station in America, if not the world.

In a very real sense Grand Central came to represent, as the New York Central liked to call it, the "Gateway to a Continent." For millions of travelers it was one of New York's most familiar buildings. The information booth at the center of Grand Central's great concourse became one of the city's best-known meeting places ("meet me under the golden clock"). The expression "like Grand Central Station" came to be synonymous with a crowded, busy public place. A trio of song writers once even set the idea to music:

"The folks call it the living room,/But lately I have learned/Tho' they call it the living room,/

As far as I'm concerned:/It's just like GRAND CENTRAL STATION/when I call on you—"*

The terminal even inspired a popular network radio drama program—"Grand Central Station"—which ran on CBS for some 20 years during the 1940's and 1950's:

"As a bullet seeks its target, shining rails in every part of our great nation are aimed at Grand Central Station, heart of the country's greatest city. Drawn by the magnetic force of the fantastic metropolis, day and night great trains rush toward the Hudson River... dive with a roar into the two-and-a-half mile tunnel beneath the swank and glitter of Park Avenue, and then—*Grand Central Station!*—Crossroads of a million private lives, gigantic stage on which are played a thousand dramas daily."

Almost from the time of its opening, the terminal's main concourse has served as a sort of unofficial public hall for New York on such diverse occasions as a 1923 memorial service for President Harding, or the 1929 unveiling of the German transatlantic airplane *Bremen,* which was placed on public exhibition hanging from the ceiling of the east balcony. Among the crowd of 15,000 at the latter event were such aviation luminaries as Clarence Chamberlain and Amelia Earhart, and the indefatigable Mayor Jimmy Walker was among the speakers. In 1931 Episcopalian Bishop William Thomas Manning opened a fund raising campaign for the cathedral of St. John the Divine with a speech from the north balcony. Thousands of people crowded the concourse on February 20, 1962, to watch on television as Col. John H. Glenn, Jr., made the first U.S. orbital space flight. CBS projected the three-orbit flight of Glenn's "Friendship 7" space craft on a giant screen. Again in 1965 a large crowd watched a similar projection of the three-orbit Gemini mission of astronauts Major Virgil I. Grissom and Lt. Cmdr. John Young. Perhaps the greatest crowd ever drawn to the concourse, however, was during the 1952 presidential campaign, when an estimated 30,000 gathered to hear President Harry Truman deliver a speech for Adlai Stevenson from a concourse balcony.

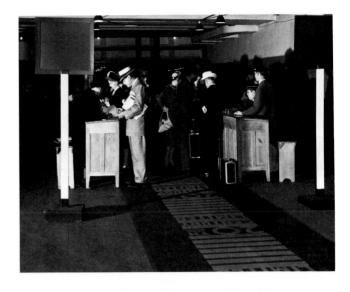

As departure time from Grand Central nears for the streamlined *Century,* passengers check in at the Pullman desk and then proceed down the handsome carpet to their assigned space within the train's gleaming gray consist.—BOTH PENN CENTRAL COMPANY.

In two typical scenes of departure time activity in Grand Central dating from April 1965 passengers board an outbound train and then a trainman waves the departure "highball." The presence of the *Creek* series 5-double bedroom-lounge-observation establishes that the train is undoubtedly the *Century*, although the red carpet is unaccountably missing.—BOTH ED NOWAK, FROM PENN CENTRAL COMPANY

Hardly less prestigious than the *Century* itself was the Central's premier train in New York-St. Louis service, the *Southwestern Limited*. The above scene of *Southwestern* departure activity at Grand Central's Track 28 dates to January 1940. (RIGHT) The long distance limiteds usually arrived in Grand Central's separate arrival station below the Biltmore Hotel. Here, a crowd has begun to gather as the *Century's* arrival time nears. (LOWER) Arrival of the *Century* was no less momentous an occasion than its departure. This crowd gathered at Grand Central's Track 26 in January 1939 for the arrival of the streamlined *Century* after its 16-hour dash from Chicago.— DAVID V. HYDE, FROM PENN CENTRAL COMPANY

It was an afternoon of high excitement on April 24, 1932, when the *Century* departed for Chicago on a new 18-hour schedule. On hand at the Grand Central festivities were New York Mayor Jimmy Walker, Mr. and Mrs. William K. Vanderbilt, Jr., and New York Central President Frederick E. Williamson. (LEFT) A favorite conveyance of the entertainment world during the 1930's was the Central's *Advance 20th Century*, a train no less elegant than the *Century* itself, complete even to the same red carpet on the Grand Central platform. Among its passengers of 1931-32, for example, we find actress Gloria Swanson.—BOTH PENN CENTRAL COMPANY

GRAND CENTRAL CELEBRITIES

In the golden years of the great limiteds an observation platform photograph in the gloom of Grand Central was a recognized badge of status and celebrityhood. In this sampling of prominent *Century* passengers, all taken in 1931, we see actress Ginger Rogers doubtlessly en route to Hollywood. (LEFT) In a variation from the customary rear platform view, opera singer Lily Pons arrives aboard the *Century* in 1940. Streamlining had eliminated the traditional platform pose. (LOWER LEFT) Singer Kate Smith and her mother pose for the New York Central publicity photographer.—ALL PENN CENTRAL COMPANY

Grand Central's main waiting room was a monumental sort of place, with its 5-foot high beamed ceiling and five great bronze chandeliers. This photograph dates from 1936.—PENN CENTRAL COMPANY

The north balcony was a tranquil place from which to observe the scurrying crowds in Grand Central's main concourse. Beams of sunlight from the clerestory lunettes above the south wall set off the flag in this dramatic 1956 scene by the Central's photographer.—PENN CENTRAL COMPANY

Regularly, too, the great concourse became a concert hall of sorts. It started in 1928 when a lady named Mary Lee Read persuaded the station master to let her play a concert with a borrowed grand piano from a concourse balcony. Mrs. Read soon became a Grand Central regular and her organ concerts for Christmas, Thanksgiving, Easter, Mother's Day, and National Music Week continued for several decades. Sometimes soloists or choral groups were featured as well.

On at least one occasion Grand Central was turned into a giant ballroom. On New Year's Eve in 1963 all train service was operated from the terminal's lower level while a huge charity ball was held in the main concourse. One of the evening's highlights, it was reported, was the emergence of bandleader Guy Lombardo and his Royal Canadians from the entrance to Track 24.

As one might expect of a public crossroads and meeting place routinely traversed by perhaps half a million people daily, Grand Central has seen its full share of the unusual, the curious, or the bizarre.

Cowboy actor Tom Mix once rode his horse, Tony, through the concourse, striking sparks from the Tennessee marble floor. Even more excitement was caused once in the early 1950's when 35 Los Angeles policemen, arriving for an American Legion convention, emerged without warning from the door of their train's baggage car on motorcycles, sirens screaming, and went thundering up the platform, into the great concourse, and up Charles Reed's convenient ramped exits to 42nd Street. It was something to attract the notice of even blasé New Yorkers, which doubtless was exactly what the Westerners intended.

On another occasion the arrival of two elephants disturbed the Grand Central routine. Too large to depart the terminal through the normal exits, the beasts had to be coaxed to kneel and creep through a taxi ramp.

A favorite Grand Central tale that comes in many variations, much like those about the selling of the Brooklyn Bridge to gullible outlanders, concerns the sale of the famous information booth in the main concourse. In 1929, they say, it actually happened. Confidence men collected $10,000 advance rent for

Among the largest crowds ever assembled on Grand Central's great concourse was this one, which gathered on March 23, 1965, to watch the televised space flight of Virgil Grissom and John Young projected on a giant screen.—PENN CENTRAL COMPANY

More typical of the crowds that periodically thronged the concourse was this gathering of parents and children as the annual summer camp season got underway on July 1, 1952.—ED NOWAK, FROM PENN CENTRAL COMPANY

INFORMATION PLEASE!

Surmounted by its splendid four-faced golden clock, Grand Central's information booth at the center of the main concourse became an established meeting place and crossroads for mid-town Manhattan. In the rush period, six experts manned the Information Center on the upper level, while another was on duty at the Commuter level. Twenty-six additional employees handled telephone inquiries. During World War II more than 14,800 questions were handled during a busy day! It took three years for an employee to thoroughly master the job of Information Man. He must be prepared for such questions as these: "What's the highest peak in the Adirondacks?" "Have you seen my wife?" "Can I take my dog on the sleeper?" "I came in on the 6:45; when does it go back?" "Is *The Wolverine* on-time?"—(ABOVE)— Ed Nowak, from Penn Central Company.

Over at the bronze booth in the middle of the main concourse, the information men calmly face a rapid fire of questions. "When is the next train to Harmon?" "How do I reach the Oyster Bar?" In this view stands a young wife waiting to ride home to White Plains with her husband after a day of shopping.—LIBRARY OF CONGRESS (LEFT) The information man directing a passenger to the commuter level.—ED NOWAK, FROM PENN CENTRAL COMPANY

In the peak years of passenger train travel the New York Central and the New Haven employed close to a hundred ticket agents to take care of their Grand Central Terminal passengers. This view of the Central's sleeping car and coach windows on the main concourse dates to 1965. (LOWER LEFT) Commuters lined up at the Central's suburban ticket windows around 1951.—BOTH ED NOWAK, FROM PENN CENTRAL COMPANY (BELOW) All passengers were required to show their tickets to the gateman before boarding through trains. During World War II more than a million passengers a year passed through each of Grand Central's 46 train gates.—PENN CENTRAL COMPANY

TICKETS

the booth from two brothers, Tony and Nick Fortunato, who planned to add it to their chain of fruit stands. The two learned of the hoax, goes the story, only when they arrived one morning with lumber and a crew of carpenters to enlarge the stand. Detectives were never able to locate the "con men," and the Fortunato brothers never did get their money back.

The terminal's police department, however, was more often concerned with such problems as lost children, runaways, or—occasionally— an abandoned baby. Crime in Grand Central, when it did occur, was more often the ordinary sort of thing—luggage theft, purse-snatching, or pickpocketing—that one would expect around a crowded railroad terminal. Once, three hoodlums attempted—unsuccessfully—to lift a $225,000 payroll from railroad offices at Grand Central. Occasionally such things as narcotics, bombs, counterfeit money, or—on one occasion—stolen art works worth $200,000, have been found among unclaimed luggage or in baggage lockers in the terminal. In 1976 a bomb and a communique of their demands placed in a subway station baggage locker at Grand Central figured in a bizarre international aircraft highjacking by Croatian nationalists. Apparently, no crime as violent as murder has ever been committed on Grand Central's premises, although people *have* been found dead in the terminal under questionable circumstances. But, as one long-time terminal policeman put it, "we never could prove it was murder."

At least two works of fiction, however, have used Grand Central as the setting for murder mysteries. Sue MacVeigh's *Grand Central Murder* (Houghton Mifflin, 1939), used the terminal's subterranean yards and passageways as a setting for its complex plot. Slater McGurk's *The Grand Central Murders* (Macmillan, 1963), made the main concourse the scene of a series of mysterious shootings of young women. In the book's final denouement those few readers who were able to stick with this very bad detective story to the end

In its role as a sort of public hall for New York, Grand Central displayed the German transatlantic airplane *Bremen* on the east balcony of the concourse in 1929. The replicas of the New York Central's first locomotive, the *DeWitt Clinton*, and its train were the main features of a transportation display that was a permanent fixture on the east balcony for many years.—PENN CENTRAL COMPANY

learned that the killer was a New York policeman, hypnotized by TV, who shot his victims through a hole in the Kodak transparency on the east balcony.

Grand Central is an enormous place, and it has always taken a huge work force to run it. Right after World War II when the terminal hit its all-time record level of 65 million passengers, and handled a daily average of

Grand Central's Travelers Aid desk was doing a brisk business when this photograph was taken, probably somewhere around the 1920's if we are to judge from the clothing styles.—PENN CENTRAL COMPANY

around 550 trains, it took close to 3,100 people with skills of every description to run Grand Central. There were the customary ticket sellers, gatemen, trainmasters, dispatchers, interlocking plant operators, and car repairmen. A total of 285 redcaps and 60 parcel room attendants were needed to take care of people's luggage. There were 45 men on the terminal police force, and two doctors to staff Grand Central's emergency hospital. A crew of 335 janitors, window washers, and charwomen was required to keep the place clean. It took 38 clerks to handle as many as 2,000 calls each hour for train reservations. A force of 16 information clerks manned the terminal's two information booths, answering as many as 20,000 questions a day. Another 41 information operators answered telephone inquiries. On one record day—July 3, 1942—they answered 17,313 calls for information.

Grand Central's locksmith and clock repairman were always popular subjects for feature story writers. The locksmith was said to have some 900,000 locks under his jurisdiction, including both those in the terminal and other nearby railroad buildings. The man who looked after the clocks had a total of some 800 clocks in his care, 158 of them in the terminal and the remainder in other railroad installations in the area.

For many years Grand Central even had its own orchestra—the Red Cap Orchestra—made up of musically inclined members of the terminal's huge force of redcaps. The 33-member orchestra often performed for special events in the terminal, and regularly played dance engagements around the city.

A long-time fixture in Grand Central's arrival station was gateman Billy Keogh, who announced arriving trains, kept the arrival bulletin board up to the minute, answered questions, and generally presided over the functioning of the arrival area.—ED NOWAK, FROM PENN CENTRAL COMPANY

A redcap force that at times approached nearly 300 in number was required to get Grand Central's passengers and their baggage to and from the trains. This squad of redcaps was ready for duty at a *Century* departure in 1941.—DAVID V. HYDE, FROM PENN CENTRAL COMPANY (LEFT) A vital member of Grand Central's behind-the-scenes work force was the terminal clock repairman, who had some 800 clocks under his care. Swiss-born Jacob Bachtold, shown here in his workshop in 1945, held the job for half a century.—ED NOWAK, FROM PENN CENTRAL COMPANY

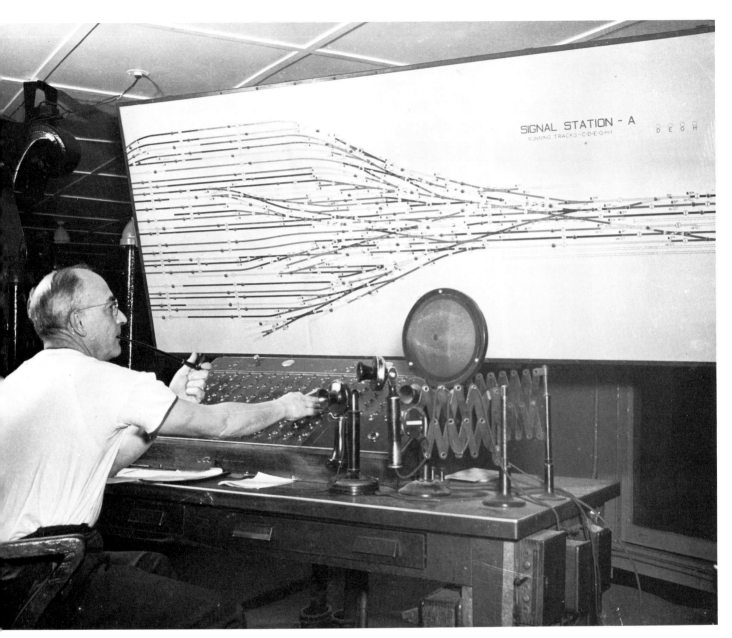

Surely one of Grand Central's most extraordinary features, and one that the public is hardly even aware of, has always been the splendidly complex system of electrically interlocked switches and signals that controls the intense flow of traffic into and out of the terminal's labyrinthine track system.

Properly speaking, the control of terminal traffic begins far north at Mott Haven, in the Bronx, where the railroad's MO Tower controls the switches and signals that gather the traffic from the separate Hudson and Harlem divisions, and funnel it down the four throat tracks that carry trains the last 5 miles into Grand Central. NK Tower, at 106th Street, can redirect trains from one to another of the four tracks. Tower U, at 57th Street, controls the flow of traffic into the terminal itself. Here the throat widens out to ten tracks. Six lead to

Grand Central's Tower A controls train movements on the terminal's upper level and the north end of the upper level loop. Train director Charles Engle was in charge of Tower A in this January 1943 scene; during a typical eight hour shift Engle and his tower crew might handle several thousand train movements.—DAVID V. HYDE, FROM PENN CENTRAL COMPANY

In a late-1950's view in Grand Central's upper level one of the New York Central's utilitarian ex-Cleveland Union Terminal box cab electric motors contrasts with the modern lines and color scheme of a New Haven FL-9, a hybrid diesel-electric design which was also capable of operating directly from the Central's third rail power supply system.—JIM SHAUGHNESSY (RIGHT) A novel view of the below-ground Grand Central is afforded by this photograph taken below 56th Street and Park Avenue, where the railroad's tracks fan out from four to ten as they approach the terminal.—RICHARD J. SOLOMON

the terminal's upper level, while four ramp down into the suburban lower level.

The great multi-level signal tower within the terminal, between 49th and 50th streets, controls almost all of the train movements within the two-level terminal. Tower A controls the upper level tracks and the north end of the loop tracks that can send trains rumbling under the Oyster Bar to reverse direction. Six men are needed to operate the tower, and they typically handle several thousand train movements during each eight-hour shift. Tower B, downstairs, controls the lower level terminal with a similar arrangement, and is only slightly less busy. Still another signal tower, Tower C under 48th Street, controls a portion of the upper level loop and a storage yard.

In the scene below, ready to depart with homeward-bound commuters, a New Haven M.U. train waits on one of Grand Central's upper level tracks.—JIM SHAUGHNESSY

TOWER
A·B

Interlocking plant operators in Grand Central's multi-level signal towers control train movements in the vast subterranean terminal. Operators in Tower A control the terminal's upper level, while those in Tower B, directly below it control Grand Central's lower level. (ABOVE) The great multi-level signal tower located between 49th and 50th streets.—ALAN GRUBER (RIGHT) Towerman working the electric switches in Tower A. (LOWER RIGHT) Another view of the electric switch machine and panel indication board. Each button tells the operator if the track is occupied and the signal designation at the switch point.—BOTH J. C. SMITH, JR.

The suburban level signal station with signal indicator board. Note the loop track board in an individual box.—J. C. SMITH, JR.

SUBURBAN COMMAND CENTER

From this "command center" in the railroad's office building at 466 Lexington Avenue, Conrail dispatchers control the flow of traffic on the former New York Central suburban routes radiating from Grand Central.—BOTH J. C. SMITH, JR.

Emerging from the gloom of the Park Avenue tunnel at 97th Street, shown on the opposite page, is New York Central's train No. 1, the all-coach New York-Chicago *Pacemaker*. Heading the train, in this 1955 scene, is class P-2a motor No. 223, a former Cleveland Union Terminal box cab locomotive.—HERBERT H. HARWOOD, JR. (RIGHT) Commuters head down the platform to a New Haven suburban train on Grand Central's lower level in the late 1950's.—JIM SHAUGHNESSY (BELOW) Class S-2 motor No. 113 handled an empty equipment train for Mott Haven at 102nd Street and Park Avenue in 1955. Even older than Grand Central itself, the enduring S motors were the Central's original electric motive power. Three still survive today.—HERBERT H. HARWOOD, JR.

COMMUTERS
COMMUTERS
COMMUTERS

Commuters, rather than the passengers of the grand limiteds, have always been the real lifesblood of Grand Central. On their way home, commuters rush for a 5:19 Brewster Local about 1951.—ED NOWAK, FROM PENN CENTRAL COMPANY (CENTER LEFT) In another scene along the Harlem River, a train of the Central's enduring M.U.'s heads west to the Hudson River suburbs in the early 1960's.—RICHARD J. SOLOMON (BELOW) Hardly less durable than the celebrated S motors were the New York Central's sturdy multiple unit suburban cars, some of which served Grand Central commuters for well over a half century. This train of the utilitarian dark green M.U.'s was westbound on the Hudson Division at Marble Hill in the Bronx in 1955.—HERBERT H. HARWOOD, JR.

Long the New York Central's principal Grand Central power were the ubiquitous T motors, which first entered service in 1913. T-2b No. 266 headed westbound train 169 at Marble Hill in 1955.—HERBERT H. HARWOOD, JR.

Normally this complex system of signals and switches is operated with well-ordered precision, but on occasion things have gone wrong.

For instance the late Herman Rinke, who spent ten years as a Grand Central towerman, recalled an occasion during the morning rush hour some years ago when a towerman up the line had routed the *20th Century Limited* down a track normally used by commuter trains. Unaware of the deviation from routine, the tower at 57th Street routed the *Century* into the lower level suburban terminal, and sent a trainload of commuters into the limited's normal track on the upper level. The startled commuters were greeted by an entire squad of redcaps, while the baggage-laden *Century* passengers found only an empty platform. As soon as it was realized what had happened, the equally startled redcaps rushed for the nearest stairway to the lower level.

There was always something out of the ordinary going on at Grand Central Terminal.

Stained with the grime of more than half a century in New York's urban environment, the Bedford Limestone walls of Grand Central loom majestically above the streetscape at 42nd Street and Park Avenue. For close to a half century the bronze figure of Commodore Vanderbilt has gazed down Park Avenue from its pedestal on Grand Central's elevated driveway. Originally erected by Vanderbilt himself atop the new St. John's Park freight station in 1869, the statue was moved to its present location in 1929.— WILLIAM D. MIDDLETON

8

What Future For Grand Central?

If the great urban complex that Grand Central generated continued to grow and prosper, the terminal itself came into difficult times in the decades that followed World War II.

Although few recognized it at the time, the great surge of traffic of World War II and the immediate postwar years was to prove the last hurrah of the long distance passenger train. Passenger traffic had long been an important part of the business of railroads like the New York Central and the New Haven, and they made substantial investments in new equipment and improved services in an endeavor to preserve it, but the decline was hardly any less precipitous for the effort. Deposed by the airplane and the automobile, Grand Central's great fleet of long distance trains dwindled away, and no longer did the rich, the powerful, and the celebrated pass through its train gates bound to and from their missions of importance. The commuters continued to come and go from Grand Central pretty much as always; nearly 40 million of them every year. But for the railroads the home-to-work trade was an increasingly profitless business.

As the New York Central's passenger fortunes

declined, it became increasingly difficult to maintain an establishment of the massive scale and opulence of Grand Central. By 1954, for example, the railroad was claiming an annual loss of $25 million on the operation of the terminal. Gradually, the structure began to show signs of age and neglect, and as the railroad sought additional sources of income for its upkeep, there were growing commercial intrusions on Grand Central's splendid public spaces.

Garish advertising displays, a stock broker's booth, auto sales agents, and similar displays of crass commercialism intruded upon the lofty grandeur of Grand Central's great concourse. Beginning in 1971 off-track horse race bets were dispensed through the ticket windows where green eye-shaded New Haven clerks once booked space on the *Merchants* or *Gilt Edge*. Indeed, what was left of the old New Haven's New England services moved downtown to Penn Station in that same year.

A jumble of telephone booths, vending machines, coin-operated baggage lockers, and kiosks robbed the terminal's waiting rooms and passageways of their dignity. Beginning in 1973 the doors of the

131

In the New York Central's financially troubled years after World War II, revenue-producing commercial displays began to intrude upon the grandeur of Grand Central's main concourse. One of the earliest major incursions was this giant, 1,080 square-foot Kodak color transparency that was installed on the east balcony in 1950.

great terminal that never closed for more than 60 years were locked during the late night hours; the legions of derelicts and panhandlers that had come to look on it as home had become too much to cope with. Grand Central had become much like some great dowager empress fallen into penury in her twilight years.

But there were some victories, too, on this road to decline. In 1949 the railroad decided to broadcast advertising over the terminal's public address system. A vociferous opposition led by the late Harold Ross, the curmudgeonly editor of *The New Yorker* magazine, finally persuaded the railroad to desist.

A decade later there was a proposal to install a 44-lane bowling alley in the vaulted space above Grand Central's elegant main waiting room. An outraged opposition prevailed in this instance, too, and the city denied the zoning change that would have been required to construct the project.

Periodically, the very survival of Grand Central itself was threatened. In 1954, soon after taking control of the railroad, New York Central Chairman Robert R. Young proposed that the terminal be razed and a new office building of more than 5 million square feet, and higher than the Empire State Building, be erected on air rights in its place. The strength of the opposition suggested the degree of public affection for the terminal. "It belongs in fact to the nation," maintained *Architectural Record* in mustering the support of an impressive array of architectural names to protest the Central's plan.

The threat passed, and so did another of a few years later, when the New York Central and the New Haven proposed to terminate their trains in Harmon and New Rochelle, respectively, and to give up their passenger operations on Manhattan altogether.

A variation of Young's scheme that was advanced soon afterward proposed the preservation of the main terminal building by placing a massive new office tower between the concourse and the New York Central Building to the north. It was better than losing Grand Central, but the design for Grand Central City, as it was initially called, generated little enthusiasm among architectural critics. Designed by architect Walter Gropius, it was to be a great tapered slab of a building, 59 stories high, that dwarfed everything else in sight and effectively blocked off any view up or down Park Avenue. Its thousands of office workers, it was feared, would bring unbearable congestion to the Grand Central District. "Not only not grand," wrote architectural critic Edgar Kaufmann, Jr. of it in *Harper's*, "it's uncomfortably out of human scale and downright ugly." But Grand Central City, renamed the Pan Am Building at the behest of its principal tenant, was built, and Grand Central Terminal managed to survive it.

Construction of the Pan Am building would seem to have ended the threat to the survival of Grand Central, but less than five years after the Pan Am opened, the Penn Central Company, which succeeded the New York Central after its 1968 merger with the Pennsylvania Railroad, was back with yet another skyscraper-over-Grand-Central plan. This time British developer Morris Saady, who had leased the air rights from Penn Central, proposed to erect a 55-story office building above the terminal. The great concourse would have been preserved, but the building's splendid facade would either have been destroyed or greatly altered.

The outcry that greeted this new scheme was

Always attentive to any compromise of the dignity of Grand Central's public spaces, *The New Yorker* magazine did not overlook the arrival of New York City's Off-Track Betting Corporation on the main concourse in 1971. The cartoon was by George Booth. — DRAWING BY BOOTH; C 1972. THE NEW YORKER MAGAZINE, INC.

"What the hell do you mean you don't sell tickets to Larchmont?"

predictable. "It's the wrong building, in the wrong place, at the wrong time," declared Donald K. Elliott, chairman of the city's planning commission. *The New York Times* critic Ada Louis Huxtable called it "a magnificently ludicrous plan." "Outrage," said architect Philip Johnson. The general public was hardly less upset than the professionals.

Much of the criticism was directed at the still greater congestion that yet another giant office building would bring to the horizontal and vertical circulation system of the Grand Central area. As Frank Williams commented in *Architectural Forum*, the new building "might well prove to be the addition that finally exhausted this remarkable mixing machine."

For many of the critics it was simply the idea of losing Grand Central's bold, if not always admired, Beaux Arts facade, which did something for the spirit that the blank slab of yet another office building could not. More practically, as some critics pointed out, Grand Central provided one of the last reservoirs of sunlight and air among the towers of its particular part of Manhattan.

Overlooked in the controversy, and no longer very relevant in any case, was the fact that just such a development had been an integral part of the architects' original plans for the terminal building. As far back as 1911, readers of *Munsey's Magazine* were shown a drawing of the huge office building that even then was planned to rise some day above the terminal.

This time the Grand Central preservationists had a strong ally in New York City's landmarks law, under which the terminal had been declared a landmark in 1967. Two different variations of the plan, both developed by architect Marcel Breuer, were presented to the city's Landmarks Preservation Commission in 1968 and 1969, and both were turned down on esthetic grounds. There was an attempt by the city to find a compromise, under which the air rights over the terminal could be transferred to nearby properties, maintaining the over-all density of the zoning district. For a time it appeared that developer Saady and the Penn Central were ready to build an alternate project under the air rights transfer scheme, but finally a decision was made to

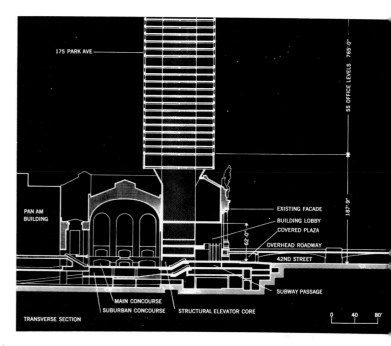

These two drawings, also from *The Architectural Forum* of July-August 1968, show how the new office tower's structural elevator core would have risen through the space between Grand Central's main concourse and the waiting room, which would have become the new building's lobby. (BELOW) A view of the planned new system of pedestrian circulation that would have served the office tower and terminal.—AUTHOR'S COLLECTION

The most recent threat to Grand Central's integrity came in the form of a 1968 proposal by developer Morris Saady that would have placed this 55-story office tower directly above the main terminal building. This drawing, from the July-August 1968 issue of *The Architectural Forum*, shows architect Marcel Breuer's initial design concept for the structure. Architectural critic Ada Louis Huxtable, never at a loss for words, called it a "magnificently ludicrous plan," and raised visions of the idea becoming a precedent for "office towers rising like funny hats over churches and mansions."—AUTHOR'S COLLECTION

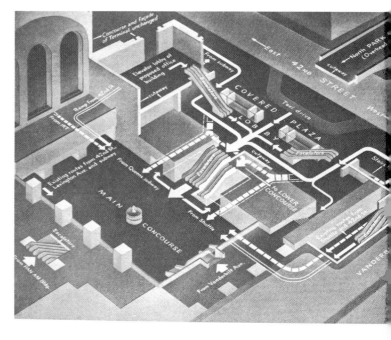

After the original "Breuer One" proposal failed to gain the required certificate of "no exterior effect" from New York City's Landmarks Preservation Commission, the architect came up with this "Breuer Two" variation which would have entirely destroyed Grand Central's exterior, but would have preserved and restored the main concourse. It, too, failed to win approval.—MARCEL BREUER & ASSOCIATES, ARCHITECTS

file suit against the landmarks law.

Joining the Landmarks Preservation Commission in what promised to be the climactic battle over Grand Central's future were the New York State Attorney General and such groups as the American Institute of Architects, the Municipal Art Society, and the newly-formed Committee to Save Grand Central Station, which was headed by former Mayor Robert F. Wagner and included among its members such notables as Jacqueline Kennedy Onassis, Bess Myerson, Jimmy Breslin, and Brendan Gill.

In January 1975 Penn Central won a decision by State Supreme Court Justice Irving H. Saypol that removed the terminal's landmark status, giving the railroad the freedom to carry out its plans. The opposition appealed and in December 1975 the decision was overturned by the State Court's Appellate Division, which found the landmarks law constitutional.

Even then, however, the battle was far from over, for by the Spring of 1977 Penn Central and its developer were back in court with an appeal to New York State's highest court, the Court of Appeals. That court, too, decided in favor of the landmarks law, leaving only an appeal to the U.S. Supreme Court as a last resort for Penn Central. Predictably, the railroad appealed and it was not until June 26, 1978, that the issue was finally decided, once and for all, when the Supreme Court, too, upheld the city's landmarks law.

With Grand Central finally saved, there now remained the almost equally difficult battle to restore the terminal to its proper magnificence. Somehow, ways had to be found to beat back the worst of the commercial intrusions and to undertake a massive renewal of Grand Central's great public spaces.

Happily, there were some encouraging beginnings. In 1972, even before the long legal battle over the terminal's landmark status had come to an end, New York's publicly-financed Metropolitan Transportation Authority had taken over operation of the terminal under a lease from Penn Central, and in 1975 the MTA had begun a million dollar program to restore and upgrade the terminal's interior. The imitation Caen stone walls were cleaned, revealing their warm, buff tones that hadn't been seen for decades. Street entrances to the terminal were repaired and cleaned, commercial booths and displays were removed from the east balcony of the main concourse, baggage lockers were banished from the main waiting room, and the grimy, cluttered passageway through the Graybar Building to Lexing-

Amtrak

The New York Central's name passenger trains of splendor and resounding title, the rich heritage left us by the Vanderbilts, were nearly all gone from the express level by the time Amtrak took over the nation's rail passenger service on May 1, 1971. The Amtrak act provided that all intercity passenger service not paid for by Amtrak could be dropped, although Penn Central and New Haven were required to continue commuter service, not included in the Amtrack system. Grand Central's upper express level saw little use except for rush hour service until Amtrak reinstated some former intercity routes that had not moved to Penn Station. (ABOVE) The first run of the new *Lake Shore Limited* from Grand Central Terminal.—AL GRUBER (LEFT) An ultra-modern visitor to Grand Central's platforms is Amtrak's new *Turboliner*, jointly built by French and U.S. firms. The train is seen here on a September 19, 1976, press run that preceded the inaugural of regular *Turbo* service to upstate New York—J. C. SMITH, JR.

Passengers stride across a Tennessee marble main concourse floor that has felt the tred of countless millions of travelers over its more than 60 years. (BELOW) Long distance travelers wait at Amtrak ticket windows in the passage between Grand Central's main waiting room and the main concourse.—BOTH J. C. SMITH, JR.

METRO

New York State's publicly-financed Metropolitan Transportation Authority took over the operation of Grand Central Terminal under a lease from Penn Central in 1972. The MTA began to renovate the structure and provide new equipment on the electrified suburban lines. (ABOVE) In the gloom of Grand Central's subterranean platforms, a New Haven line train waits for commuters.—JANE F. GOLDSMITH (LEFT) Arriving commuters from a New Haven train stream down the platforms. (BELOW) By mid-morning, crowds on the suburban concourse have thinned noticeably.—BOTH J. C. SMITH, JR.

ton Avenue was cleared and refurbished. In 1976 the MTA began illuminating the Coutan statuary group on the building's 42nd Street facade for the first time since the terminal had opened.

A much greater restoration effort lay ahead for Grand Central. The former New York Central and New Haven commuter services using the terminal had passed from the bankrupt Penn Central to newly-formed Conrail in 1976, and then to a new MTA public agency, Metro-North Commuter Railroad, as of January 1, 1983. With the commuter rail properties came operating control of Grand Central, and the new agency soon began an ambitious program to preserve and restore the building.

A first major project in the restoration carried out during 1986-87 was reconstruction of the building's badly deteriorated roof. Some 60,000 square feet of copper roofing and the building's elaborate, copper clad decorative fascia were replaced or repaired. Thirteen skylights that had illuminated the public areas of the terminal until they were covered over during World War II were repaired and reopened.

With Grand Central once again watertight, Metro-North began planning a comprehensive restoration effort for the terminal's interior spaces. In 1988 a consortium of architectural and engineering firms headed by New York architects Beyer Blinder Belle, who had planned the restoration of Ellis Island, was commissioned to develop a master plan for a major restoration and renovation of the terminal and its utilities systems that would preserve and restore the architecture and art work, improve and expand the building's retail spaces, and enhance its function as a transportation center. A year later Metro-North selected retail specialist Williams Jackson Ewing to prepare a master plan for retail development within the terminal.

By 1990 the MTA had adopted a comprehensive master plan for the restoration of Grand Central, and authorized $160 million in utility upgrades, structural repairs, and improvements for the main concourse. By 1992 the main waiting room had been fully restored. No longer required for long distance rail passengers, the handsome room, now called Vanderbilt Hall, took on a new function as an exhibition and special event space. A year later the Vanderbilt Avenue taxi stand and entrance had been restored.

By 1994 the MTA had gained long-term control of Grand Central through a 110-year lease from Penn Central successor American Premier Under-

writers, Inc., and in 1996 work finally began on a two-year, $197 million major restoration and improvement program for the main concourse and other public spaces. Utilities systems were rebuilt or replaced, and the entire building was air conditioned for the first time. Seven new elevators and six new escalators were installed, and main entrance passageways from 42nd Street and the subways were widened and regraded to improve circulation.

An entirely new entrance established at 43rd Street and Lexington Avenue, on the east side of the terminal, incorporated a link to Grand Central's past. Recovered from the garden of a Bronxville home, a ton-and-a-half cast iron eagle that had once perched on one of the towers of the 1898 Grand Central Station was refurbished and placed above the new entrance.

The most visible improvements were in the main concourse itself. An early part of the work was a restoration of the celebrated sky ceiling. The cer-

No longer particularly relevant to the controversy surrounding Grand Central's future was the original plan of its architects, who contemplated this 23-story office building above the concourse. The structural framework of the terminal was designed to support the later addition of the office structure. The drawing is from the April 1911 issue of *Munsey's Magazine*.—LIBRARY OF CONGRESS

This inscription over Grand Central's main entrance honors the terminal's builders.—Ed Nowak, from Penn Central Company

ulean blue ceiling itself was cleaned for the first time in more than 50 years, plaster surrounds and arches were cleaned and recoated, and 60 principal stars in the constellation were illuminated by a new fiber-optic lighting system. Between the concourse and the main waiting room to the south, office space constructed above the ramps to the lower level in 1927 was removed, opening up again the view of the sky ceiling. A new Botticino marble staircase to the balcony on the east side of the main concourse, planned by the original architects but never built, was put in place opposite the west staircase. Quarries were reopened and stone workers flown in from Italy to obtain replacement sections of pink Tennessee marble for the concourse floor.

Much of the financing for the terminal's restoration would come from retail development, through an $84 million bond issue that would be repaid from future rental income. Grand Central's retail development team produced a plan for a balanced mixture of retail and dining establishments in the terminal, almost doubling retail space from 105,000 square feet to a total of 170,000 square feet for more than a hundred shops and restaurants. New restaurants were opened on the east balcony overlooking the main concourse, a dining concourse was established on the lower level, and food stalls were installed in a Grand Central Market along the new

entranceway from Lexington Avenue.

Substantial completion of the restoration was celebrated in grand style on October 1, 1998. Politicians spoke, an orchestra played the specially commissioned march "Grand Central," accompanied by six Metro-North trainmen on bells, whistles, and a box and ratchet contraption that simulated the sound of train wheels. A mariachi band marched, a trapeze artist performed, and a laser light show played on the newly-restored sky ceiling..

While Grand Central's very future was being resolved, the nature of the terminal's rail traffic was undergoing fundamental changes. A declining volume of intercity rail traffic through Grand Central had been further reduced with the formation of Amtrak in 1971. What remained of the former New Haven's New England services shifted to the Hell Gate Bridge route and Penn Station, leaving only services to Montreal, Chicago, and Upstate New York operating from Grand Central. Even these trains disappeared in 1991, when Amtrak completed a new west side connection along the Hudson River and began operating all of its New York services from Penn Station.

Grand Central was now exclusively a commuter terminal, but it was a traffic that was growing more important all the time. The New York Central and New Haven services that used Grand Central had

Restoration of Grand Central's main concourse included cleaning of the famous sky ceiling and refurbishing of its elaborate plaster arches and surrounds. Early in 1997, a workman recoated ornamental plaster work in the ceiling arches. (BELOW) A major improvement included in the main concourse restoration was the addition of a Botticino marble staircase on the east side, opposite the original west side staircase, that had been planned in the original design but was never completed. This view shows the new staircase under construction in October 1997. — BOTH JAMES RUDNICK PHOTOGRAPHY

suffered a long decline into disrepair as the fortunes of the two railroads ebbed in the years after World War II. Things only grew worse after the ill-fated Penn Central merger of 1968, and the dilapidated commuter lines finally emerged as part of the new federally-created Conrail in 1976. By this time some public funding was beginning to flow to support the commuter services, and the next step came at the beginning of 1981, when the MTA's new Metro-North Commuter Railroad assumed ownership and operation of the commuter lines north of New York City and began a massive rehabilitation and improvement program for the Grand Central commuter services.

Over the next decade Metro-North turned around the decline of its commuter system with new equipment; rehabilitated track, signal, and power systems; new and improved stations; and expanded services. By 1997 Metro-North traffic hit a record high of 62.6 million annual passengers, most of then traveling to or from Grand Central. With all of these commuters, together with all of the other pedestrian traffic through the terminal, a half million people were passing through Grand Central every day.

Early in 1999, Metro-North completed a $113 million project that significantly expanded Grand Central's remarkable system of subterranean pedestrian passageways and further enhanced the terminal's capacity to support a growing Metro-North traffic. By opening up new entrances to the north, the project provides more direct access between the Grand Central platforms and work destinations for an estimated 40,000 daily passengers who work north of the terminal. A system of new staircases, escalators, and elevators connects the upper and lower platform levels with new east-west cross platform connections at 45th and 47th streets. These, in turn, are linked with two new north-south pedestrian spines at the upper platform level that carry pedestrians to new street entrances in the archways of the Helmsley Building on Park Avenue, at 47th Street and Madison Avenue, and at 48th Street and Park Avenue.

As the end of the century drew near, an even greater role in regional transportation was in store for this remarkable terminal as planners began to look at innovative ways to accommodate the transportation needs of the growing New York metropolitan area. A visionary 1993 report of the Regional Plan Association proposed the development of a Regional Express Rail (Rx) system for the tri-state, 31-county New York Metropolitan area that would require new links between the region's existing rail lines and the two Manhattan terminals to permit regional services through-routed over Metro-North, LIRR, and New Jersey Transit lines. Two other major planning studies proposed specific new links to Grand Central that could help to realize this vision of a regional rail network.

At the end of 1998 MTA Long Island Rail Road was in the midst of preliminary engineering and environmental studies leading to construction of a 10-year, $3.2 billion East Side Access project that would bring an estimated 172,000 daily LIRR passengers through Grand Central. Designed to relieve congestion at the LIRR's present Penn Station terminal in Manhattan and to provide a more direct service for Long Island commuters enroute to and from east side destinations, the long-planned project would bring Long Island trains into Manhattan through the lower level of the MTA's 63rd Street tunnel under the East River. Nearly two miles of tunneling through earth or hard rock in Queens and Manhattan would link LIRR's Main Line and Port Washington Branch with the East River tunnel and a new 10-track, five-platform LIRR terminal on Grand Central's lower level.

A further expansion of Grand Central's role as a transportation center was forecast by an Access to the Region's Core study completed by the Port Authority of New York and New Jersey, the MTA, and NJ Transit in 1998. Among its proposals for improved regional transportation, the study recommended construction of a tunnel between Penn Station and Grand Central, an idea that has been around ever since the two terminals were completed early in the century. The connection would permit NJ Transit trains to operate through to Grand Central, providing direct service to Manhattan's east side from New Jersey, while Metro-North trains could continue on from Grand Central to provide direct service to the Penn Station area from the north. The tunnel would also enable the three New York commuter rail carriers to operate through-routed regional services much like those proposed by the 1993 regional plan.

Considering the history of this extraordinary work wrought by the genius of Wilgus, Reed, and Warren, there can be little doubt that Grand Central Terminal can once again successfully adapt to meet new needs of the city it has served so well for more than 85 years. For, as always with Grand Central, the possibilities are almost endless.

Appendix

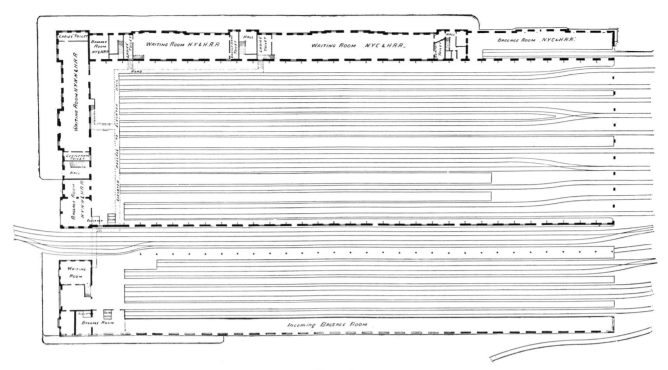

Figure 1

Plan of the original Grand Central Depot complex, with the Annex of 1885-1886.—DONALD
DUKE COLLECTION

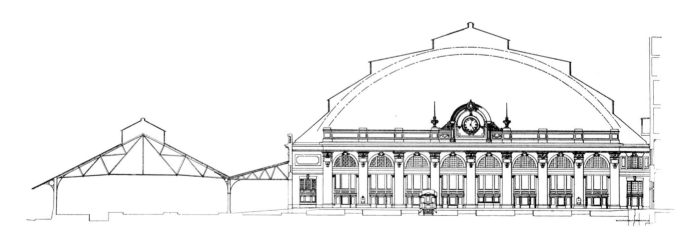

Figure 2

The arrangement of the reconstructed Grand Central Station of 1898-1900 is shown here in a
cross-sectional drawing from *The Railroad Gazette*.—DONALD DUKE COLLECTION

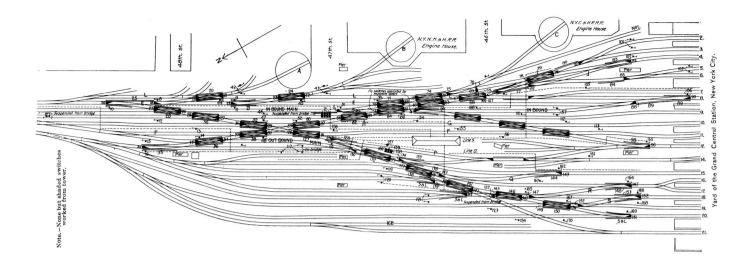

Figure 3

A station track plan of the reconstructed Grand Central Station of 1898-1900 as it appeared in the June 23, 1899 issue of *The Railroad Gazette.*—DONALD DUKE COLLECTION

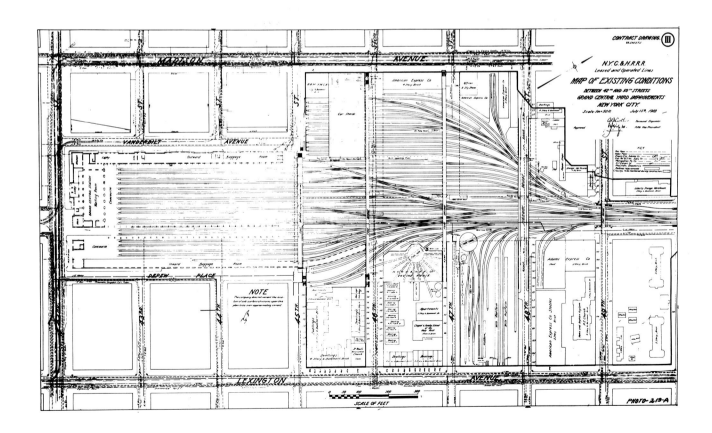

Figure 4

The layout of the terminal yard in July 1903, just before work started on the new Grand Central Terminal.—HERBERT H. HARWOOD COLLECTION

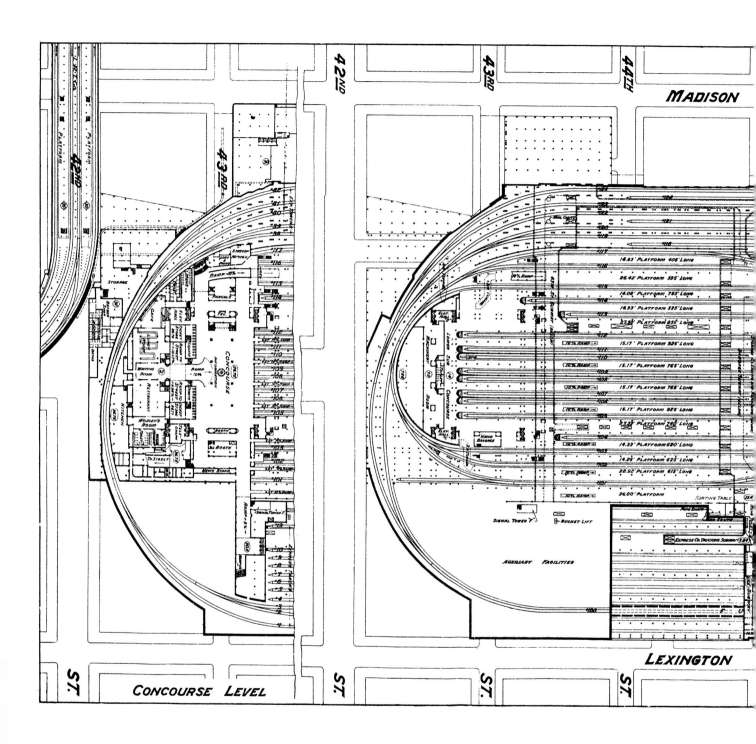

MADISON

42ND

43RD

44TH

14.63' PLATFORM 405' LONG
26.42' PLATFORM 535' LONG
14.08' PLATFORM 785' LONG
14.33' PLATFORM 525' LONG
27.50' PLATFORM 855' LONG
15.17' PLATFORM 925' LONG
15.17' PLATFORM 765' LONG
15.17' PLATFORM 765' LONG
15.17' PLATFORM 925' LONG
27.33' PLATFORM 760' LONG
14.33' PLATFORM 620' LONG
14.25' PLATFORM 625' LONG
22.92' PLATFORM 615' LONG
26.00' PLATFORM

SORTING TABLE

SIGNAL TOWER "F"   BUCKET LIFT

AUXILIARY   FACILITIES

EXPRESS CO. TRUCKING SUBWAY

LEXINGTON

CONCOURSE LEVEL

ST.   ST.   ST.   ST.

CONCOURSE

STORAGE

PARCELS

CAFE

WAITING ROOM

RESTAURANT

KITCHEN

WOMEN'S ROOM

TO STREET

NEWS STAND

SIGNAL TOWER "F"

RAMP 10%

ELEV. HALL

CONCOURSE

HAND BAGGAGE

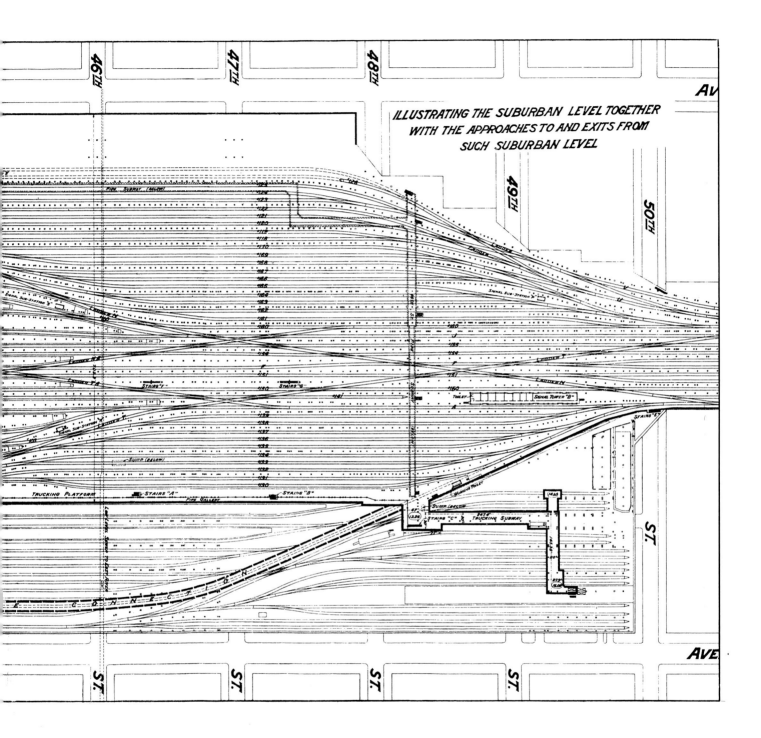

Figure 5

Grand Central Terminal's Suburban Train Level Plan.—HERBERT H. HARWOOD COLLECTION

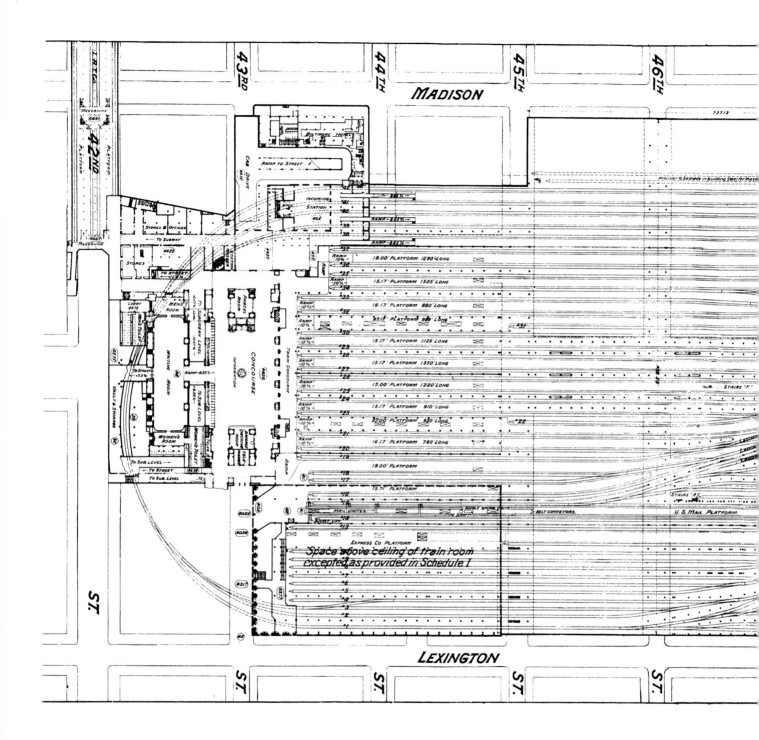

Space above ceiling of train room
excepted, as provided in Schedule 1

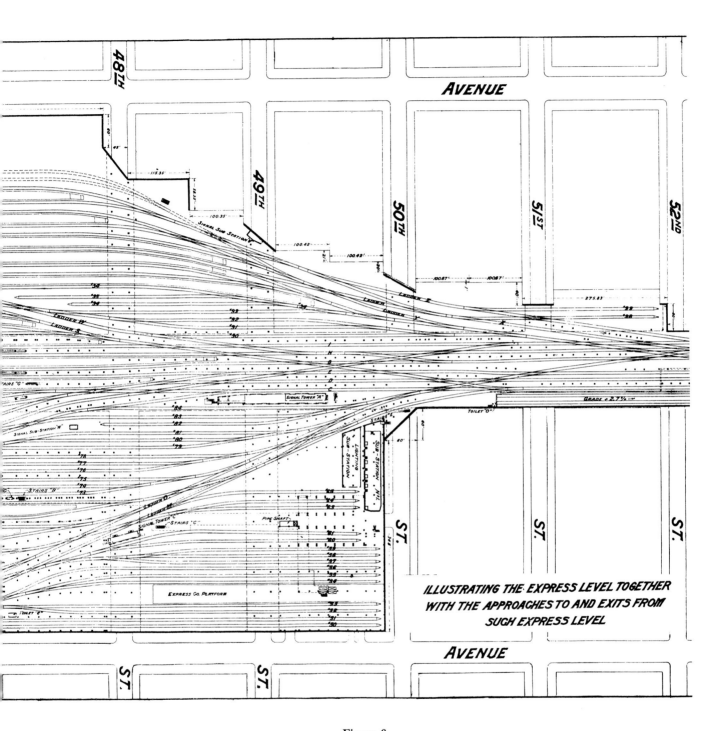

Figure 6

Grand Central Terminal's Express Train Level Plan.—Herbert H. Harwood Collection

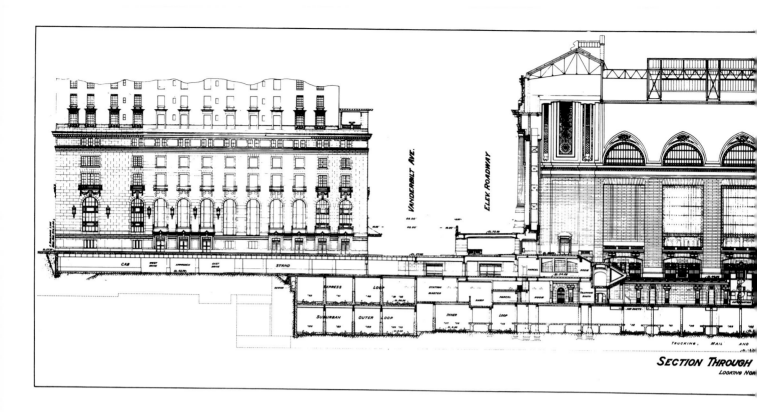

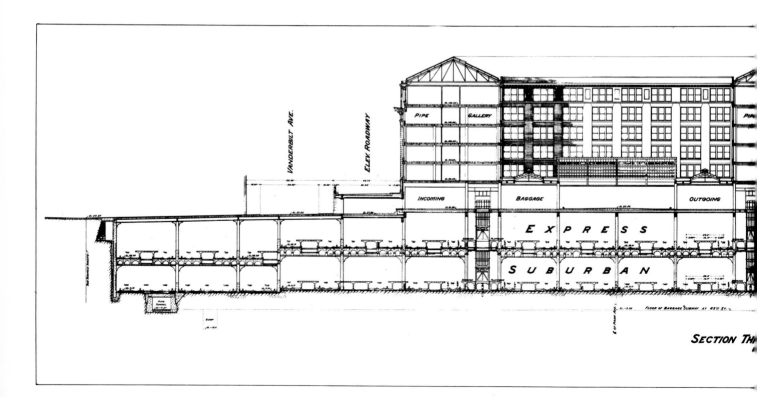

Figure 8

Grand Central Terminal, Cross Section through 44th Street, June 1912.—HERBERT H. HAR-
WOOD COLLECTION

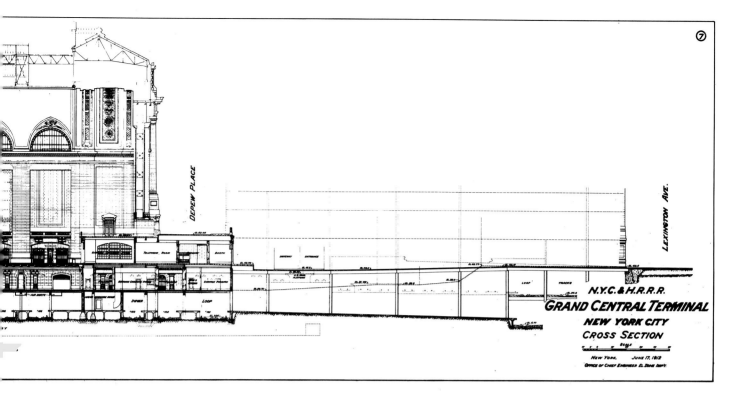

Figure 7

Grand Central Terminal, Cross Section through 43rd Street, June 1912.—HERBERT H. HAR-
WOOD COLLECTION

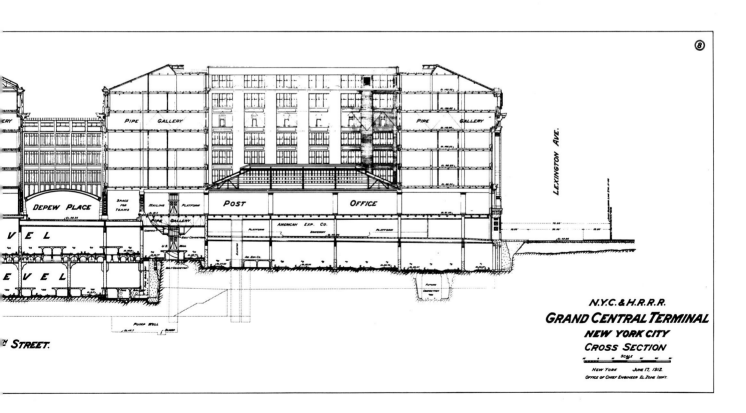

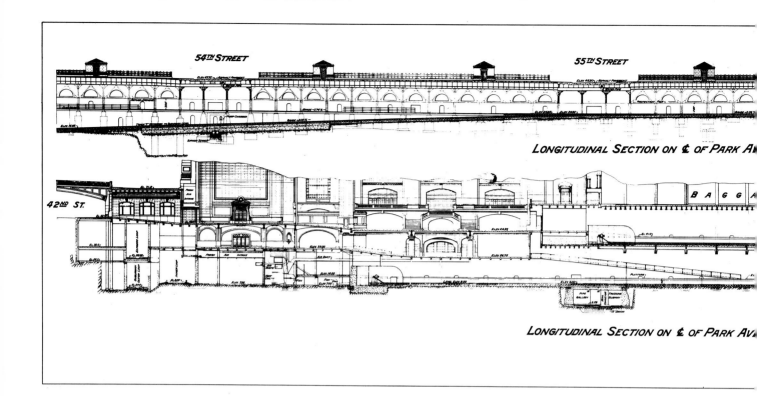

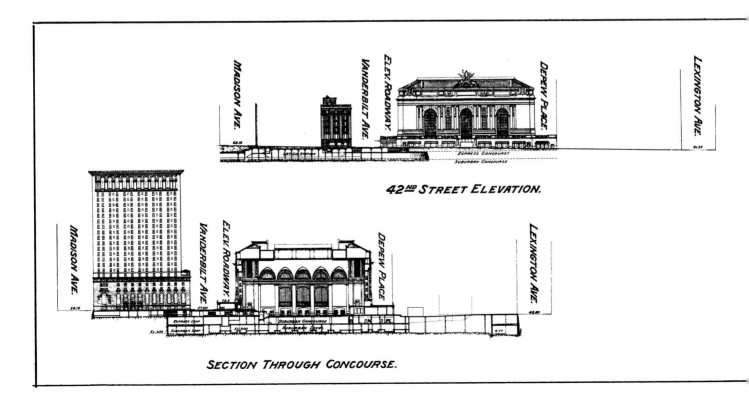

Figure 10

Grand Central Terminal, Longitudinal Section on Park Avenue, 42nd Street Elevation, and
Section Through Concourse, June 1912—HERBERT H. HARWOOD COLLECTION

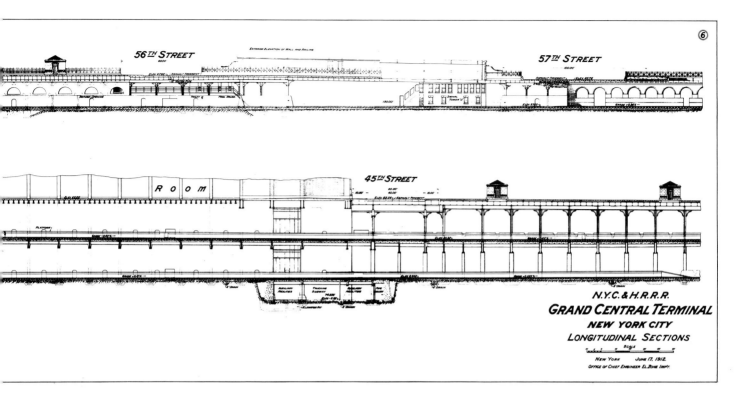

Figure 9

Grand Central Terminal, Longitudinal Section Along Park Avenue Centerline, June 1912.—
HERBERT H. HARWOOD COLLECTION

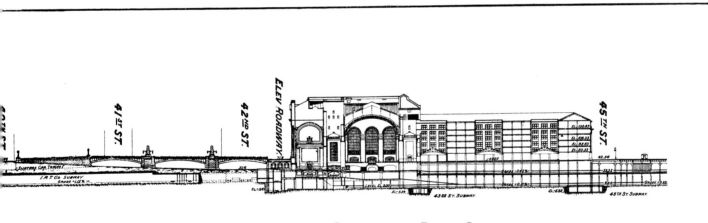

LONGITUDINAL SECTION ON PARK AVENUE.

ILLUSTRATING CROSS SECTIONS AND
LONGITUDINAL SECTION

GRAND CENTRAL TERMINAL

Bibliography

The following is a summary of the principal reference sources for this book, as well as additional published materials which are recommended for further reading on the subject of the Grand Central Terminal and its predecessors.

"A Gateway to the Heart of New York." *Scientific American Supplement,* Vol. 74 (Dec. 7, 1912), pp. 364-366.

"A Great Subterranean Railway Junction." *Scientific American,* Vol. 103 (Nov. 19, 1910), pp. 393, 398.

Barnett, Jonathan, *Urban Design as Public Policy.* New York, Architectural Record Books. 1974.

Beebe, Lucius, *20th Century.* Berkeley, Calif., Howell-North Books, 1962.

Bernard, Walter, "The World's Greatest Railway Terminal." *Scientific American,* Vol. 104 (June 17, 1911), pp. 594-595, 609-610.

Birmingham, Frederic A., "Grand Central Station." *Holiday,* Vol. 44 (Aug., 1968), pp. 26-29, 75-76.

"Can the Grand Central Concourse be saved." *The Architectural Forum,* Vol. 101 (Nov., 1954), pp. 134-139.

Carley, Clyde, "This is Grand Central." *Railway Progress,* Vol. 11 (May, 1957) pp. 4-9.

"Columns in the New Grand Central Terminal, New York City." *Engineering Record,* Vol. 67 (Feb. 1, 1913), pp. 125-126.

Condit, Carl W., *American Building Art.* New York, Oxford University Press, 1960, 1961, 2 vols.

"Congestion of Traffic at the Grand Central Station and its Remedy." *Scientific American,* Vol. 83 (Dec. 1, 1900), p. 338.

Coombs, Robert, "42nd." *The Livable City,* Vol. 3 (April, 1976), pp. 1-4.

Curran, Arthur, "Yesterdays at the Grand Central." Bulletin No. 35, Railway & Locomotive Historical Society, 1934, pp. 79-83.

Donovan, Francis D., "Grand Central Station and its Predecessors." *The Railway History Monograph,* Vol. 3 (Oct. 1974), pp. 65-87.

Droege, John A., *Passenger Terminals and Trains.* New York, McGraw-Hill Co., Inc., 1916. Reprint edition, Milwaukee, Kalmbach Publishing Co., 1969.

Edwards, H.R., "Colossus of Roads." *Railroad Stories,* Vol. 20 (Nov., 1936), pp. 4-23.

"Engineer for N. Y. Central Tells How an Idle Sketch Led to Gigantic Terminal." *New York Telegram,* Feb. 22, 1929.

Fischer, Edward G., with Amos, Wayne, "Everything Happens at Grand Central Station." *Collier's* Vol. 133 (Mar. 5, 1954), pp. 86-89.

Fitch, James Marston, and Waite, Diana S., *Grand Central Terminal and Rockefeller Center; A Historic-critical Estimate of Their Significance.* New York, New York State Parks & Recreation, Division for Historic Preservation, 1974.

Fowler, Glenn, "Grand Central May Get a Tower." *The New York Times,* Sept. 21, 1967.

——— "Grand Central Proposal Scored." *The New York Times,* Sept. 22, 1967.

——— "Grand Central Tower Will Top Pan Am Building." *The New York Times,* June 20, 1968, pp. 1, 36.

"Girders in the Grand Central Terminal, New York City." *Engineering Record,* Vol. 67 (Jan. 18, 1913), pp. 78-79.

"Grand Central City." *The Architectural Forum,* Vol. 129 (July-Aug., 1968), pp. 72-73.

"Grand Central Depot Signal System." *Scientific American,* Vol. 33 (Dec. 25, 1875), pp. 399, 402.

"Grand Central Interlocking Machine." *Railway Age Gazette,* Vol. 50 (May 12, 1911), pp. 1115-1116.

"Grand Central's Outdoor Concourse." *The Architectural Forum,* Vol. 102 (Feb., 1955), pp. 116-119.

"Grand Central Station Improvements and Connection With Rapid Transit Subway." *Scientific American,* Vol. 88 (Jan. 17, 1903), pp. 39-40.

Grand Central Terminal. New York, New York Central RR, ca. 1912.

Grand Central Terminal. New York, New York Central RR, ca. 1965.

Harlow, Alvin F., *The Road of the Century; The Story of the New York Central.* New York, Creative Age Press, 1947.

Haskell, Douglas, "The Lost New York of the Pan American Airways Building." *The Architectural Forum,* Vol. 119 (Nov., 1963), pp. 106-111.

Hendrick, Burton J., "The Vanderbilt Fortune." *McClure's Magazine,* Vol. 32 (Nov., 1908), pp. 46-62.

Holton, James L., "Grand Central Terminal Rapidly Nears its Capacity, Engineers Studying Means to End Commuter Jams." *New York Telegram,* Feb. 2, 1929, pp. 1, 5.

Horsley, Carter B., "City Appeal a Key Test of Policy on Landmarks." *The New York Times,* Oct. 12, 1975, Section R, pp. 1, 8.

———— "Grand Central Getting a $1-Million Facelift." *The New York Times,* Aug. 31, 1975, Section R, pp. 1, 6.

Hungerford, Edward, *Men and Iron; The History of the New York Central.* New York, Thomas Y. Crowell Co., 1938.

———— "The Greatest Railway Terminal in the World." *The Outlook,* Vol. 102 (Dec. 28, 1912), pp. 900-911.

Huxtable, Ada Louis, "Progressive Architecture in America: Grand Central Depot—1869-71." *Progressive Architecture,* Vol. 37 (Oct., 1956), pp. 135-138.

———— "The Stakes Are High for All in Grand Central Battle," *The New York Times,* Apr. 11, 1969, p. 28.

"Improvement of the Grand Central Station, New York." *The Railroad Gazette,* Vol. 31 (June 23, 1899), pp. 447-449.

Inglis, William, "New York's New Gateway." *Harper's Weekly,* Vol. 57 (Feb. 1, 1913), pp. 13, 20.

Jacobs, Warren, "Some Railroad Landmarks of New York City." Bulletin No. 65, Railway & Locomotive Historical Society, 1944, pp. 76-82.

————"The Old Hudson River Railroad Depot and Abraham Lincoln In New York." Bulletin No. 55, Railway & Locomotive Historical Society, 1941, pp. 36-45.

Kalmbach, A. C., "Grand Central." *Trains,* Vol. 3 (Mar., 1943), pp. 8-19.

Kaufmann, Edgar, Jr., "The Biggest Office Building Yet . . . Worse Luck." *Harper's Magazine,* Vol. 220 (May, 1960), pp. 64-70.

Marshall, David, *Grand Central.* New York, Whittlesey House, 1946.

Meeks, Carroll L. V., *The Railroad Station.* New Haven, Yale University Press, 1956.

Middleton, William D., "The Grandest Terminal of Them All." *Trains,* Vol. 35 (May, 1975), pp. 22-35.

———— *When the Steam Railroads Electrified.* Milwaukee, Kalmbach Publishing Co., 1974.

"Monumental Gateway to a Great City." *Scientific American,* Vol. 107 (Dec. 7, 1912), pp. 475, 484-489, 499-501.

Mumford, Lewis, "The Sky Line: The Roaring Traffic's Boom—I." *The New Yorker,* Vol. 31 (Mar. 19, 1955), pp. 115-121.

Myers, Debs, "Grand Central Terminal." *Holiday,* Vol. 13 (Mar., 1953), pp. 64-68, 70, 72-73, 131, 133-134.

"New Grand Central Terminal Station." *Scientific American,* Vol. 99 (Dec. 5, 1908), pp. 410-412, 417, 418.

"New York Central Office Building." *The Railway Age,* Vol. 43 (Feb. 8, 1907), p. 182.

"Opening of the New Grand Central Terminal, New York City." *Engineering Record,* Vol. 67 (Feb. 8, 1913), pp. 144-148.

"Opening of the New Grand Central Terminal, New York." *Railway Age Gazette,* Vol. 54 (Feb. 7, 1913), pp. 235, 258-259.

Pope, Robert Anderson, "Grand Central Terminal Station, New York." *The Town Planning Review,* University of Liverpool Vol. 2 (April, 1911), pp. 55-64.

"Progress at the Grand Central Terminal." *Railway Age Gazette,* Vol. 49 (Sept. 16, 1910), pp. 503-507.

"Progress on the Grand Central Terminal." *Railway Age Gazette,* Vol. 53 (Nov. 22, 1912), pp. 981-986.

"Refacing the Grand Central Station Walls." *The Engineering Record,* Vol. 37 (Jan. 15, 1898), p. 146.

"Remodeling the Grand Central Station, New York." *The Engineering Record,* Vol. 40 (June 17, 1899), pp. 56-58.

"Signalling at the New Grand Central Terminal." *Railway Age Gazette,* Vol. 49 (Oct. 7, 1910), pp. 620-624.

"Solving Greatest Terminal Problem of the Age." *The New York Times,* Feb. 2, 1913, Section T.

"Some Engineering Features of the Grand Central Station, New York." *The Engineering Record,* Vol. 43 (Feb. 23, 1901), pp. 181-184.

Stem, Allen H., and Fellheimer, Alfred, *Inception and Creation of the Grand Central Terminal.* New York, privately printed, 1913.

Stuart, Inglis, "The New York and New Haven, the Hartford and New Haven, and the Western Massachusetts Railroads." Bulletin No. 12, Railway & Locomotive Historical Society, 1926, pp. 43-51.

"The Enlargement of the Grand Central Station," New York, N.Y., *Engineering News,* Vol. 39 (Jan. 6, 1898), pp. 12-14.

The Gateway to a Continent. New York, New York Central RR, ca. 1938.

"The Grand Central Station Improvements." *Scientific American,* Vol. 93 (Sept. 16, 1905), pp. 213, 222-223.

"The Grand Central Station, New York." *Architects' & Builders' Magazine,* Vol. 2 (Mar., 1901), pp. 201-208.

"The Grand Central Terminal." *Fortune,* Vol. 3 (Feb., 1931), pp. 97-99.

"The Grand Central Terminal, New York." *Railway Age Gazette,* Vol. 54 (Feb. 14, 1913), pp. 279-284.

"The Improvement of Fourth Avenue." *Frank Leslie's Illustrated Newspaper,* Vol. 35 (Feb. 15, 1873), pp. 370-372.

"The New Grand Central Station, New York." *Scientific American,* Vol. 92 (Jan. 21, 1905), pp. 40, 46.

"The New Grand Central Terminal Station in New York City: An Underground Double-Deck Terminal." *Engineering News,* Vol. 69 (May 1, 1913), pp. 883-895.

"The Proposed Tunnel Loop at the Grand Central Station." *The Railroad Gazette,* Vol. 34 (Jan. 31, 1902), p. 71.

"The Reconstruction of the Grand Central Station, New York." *The Engineering Record,* Vol. 41 (Apr. 28, 1900), pp. 398-399.

"The Revised Grand Central Station, New York City." *The Railroad Gazette,* Vol. 29 (Feb. 19, 1897), pp. 126-128.

The Sky Ceiling of Grand Central Terminal, New York. New York, New York Central RR, ca. 1942.

Thompson, Hugh, "The Greatest Railroad Terminal in the World." *Munsey's Magazine,* Vol. 45 (Apr., 1911), pp. 27-40.

Tucker, George W., *The Harlem Railroad Improvements in Manhattan.* Unpublished Master of Regional Planning thesis, Cornell University, 1961.

Wagner, Walter F., Jr., "The wrong criticism, in the wrong place, at the wrong time." *Architectural Record,* Vol. 144 (Aug., 1968), pp. 9-10.

Walker, C. Lester, "Meet Me at Grand Central." *The American Mercury,* Vol. 70 (June, 1950), pp. 689-695.

Wilgus, William J., "The Electrification of the Suburban Zone of the New York Central and Hudson River Railroad in the Vicinity of New York City," *Transactions of the American Society of Civil Engineers,* Vol. 61 (Dec., 1908), pp. 73-155.

———— "The Grand Central Terminal in Perspective." *Transactions of the American Society of Civil Engineers,* Vol. 106 (1941), pp. 992-1051.

———— Unpublished manuscripts and papers on deposits in the Manuscripts and Archives Division of the New York Public Library.

Williams, Frank, "Grand Central City." *The Architectural Forum,* Vol. 128 (Jan.-Feb., 1968), pp. 48-55.

Williams, Jesse Lynch, "The Gates of the City." *The Century Magazine,* Vol. 74 (Aug., 1907), pp. 487-500.

Index

GRAND CENTRAL T

Sectional View from Biltmore Hotel Looking East

SHOWING PASSAGEWAYS TO HOTELS, C

① — Hotel Commodore

② — Biltmore Hotel

③ — Hotel Roosevelt

④ — New York Central Bldg. —230 Park Ave.

⑤ — Graybar Building

⑥ — Grand Central Terminal Office Building

Ⓐ — Cab Baggage Service

Ⓑ — Travel Information Bur

Ⓒ — Newsreel Theatre

Ⓓ — Lower Level

Ⓔ — Stairways from Vande Ave. to Upper & Lo Levels

Ⓕ — Ticket Offices

— TO INCOMING TRAINS —

RESS TRAINS

URBAN TRAINS